MUL
FAMILY N

for
Ancestor Hunters
by
Jo Currie

Illustrations by Pat James

Brown & Whittaker
1998
Reprinted 2001, 2003

Published by Brown & Whittaker Publishing
Tobermory PA75 6PR

Text © Jo Currie 1998
Illustrations © Pat James 1998

*The author wishes to acknowledge the
following sources of information:
* General Register Office, Edinburgh,
for censuses, Old Parish Registers and
Civil Registrations.
*Inhabitants of the Argyll Estate, 1779
ed. Eric Cregeen. SRS Edinburgh, 1963
* Scottish Record office GD174
Papers of the Maclaines of Lochbuie*

ISBN 0 9528428 8 2

Set in Times New Roman 10pt and printed by Nevisprint, Scotland

PREFACE

I have selected the fifty names which were most current in Mull, Iona and Ulva between 1750 and 1850. During this time, a large number of Mull people left their overpopulated homeland not only for America, Canada, Australia and New Zealand, but also for the south of Scotland and England. American emigrants were the earliest, and they were often self sufficient and enterprising people of the tacksman class who chose emigration for the betterment of their families and the better use of their education and talents. This emigration was interrupted only briefly by the American Revolution of 1775, and resumed again in the last twenty years of the 18th century. In the first quarter of the 19th century it is not so easy to characterise the social groups leaving Mull, as there were only a few private estate censuses, or rental lists from which one can draw information of a negative kind - for instance, from lists of tenants given notice to quit for non-payment of rents. Couples who began by showing the familiar pattern of producing a child every second year, and who then disappear from baptism records, may have left the island, but might also have ceased to multiply because of the death of one of the parents. Deaths were mostly unrecorded, and only a very few gravestones testify to a tiny proportion of actual deaths. It is only with the introduction of the official, detailed, ten yearly census in 1841 that we can establish the exodus from Mull of particular families in the 19th century.

But where emigration was concerned, a new and interesting feature was emerging in these years. Several factors combined to ensure that whole families of the same name, related families of different names, and entire townships made up of people often closely related, moved out en masse. In some cases they were evicted so that 'improvements' in agriculture could be made without the 'burden' of the people. In others, rents were repeatedly raised above the means of the people, who read the writing on the wall, and chose to leave before it was too late. By the 1850s, emigration was becoming organised, and bodies such as the Highland and Island Emigration Society assisted emigration to Australia. The tendency for groups from the same estates or townships to go together prolonged kinship links into the first exiled generations, and ancestor hunters should be encouraged to look for blood ties within groups of first generation settlers overseas. Towards the end of the 19th century, emigration became again a matter of choice, and Mull people leaving in these years are usually well recorded in a series of censuses and civil registrations. The most commonly found names in Mull follow closely the history of the island itself. The oldest ones, Mackinnon, Macdonald and Macdougall, reflect the dominance of these clans before the ousting of the Lords of the Isles (who were Macdonalds). The Macleans, first merely the recipients of land grants from the Lords of the Isles in the 14th century, began to take over the power base of the Macdonalds in the 16th century, but the clan followers of the old supremacies remained on the island. The long struggles between Macleans and Campbells resulted in the exile of the Duart Macleans in 1679, and Campbell followers of the earls, and later the dukes, of Argyll, were planted in Mull to ensure the good behaviour of the now subordinate families. The Campbells first made their appearance as tacksmen (literally men who were awarded a 'tack' of land for which they paid rent, and who collected rents from resident small farmers and subtenants). Owing to the characteristic tolerance of Mull people for incomers, this arrangement was not always an unhappy one. There were marriages between Macleans and Campbells, and the dukes of Argyll did not at first force out the Maclean tacksmen. If anything, the second duke became more suspicious of his own Campbell tacksmen than those of the native breeds, and already, by the time of the 1745 uprising, he had dismissed some of his own clan on the grounds that they intercepted some of the rent monies due to him. After the '45, the third, fourth and fifth dukes reinstated Campbell tacksmen to safeguard the island against further disloyal uprisings against the house of Hanover. Mull men had not taken much part in the Jacobite rising, discouraged by the practical good sense of the Lochbuie and other Maclean branches, but Macleans from the mainland had been involved in the rebel cause, and a great deal of sympathy and support, expressed in pro-Jacobite songs and poetry, lay under the surface of 18th century Mull life.

In the last quarter of the 18th century, therefore, we find the island principally populated by the old names, Mackinnon, Macgillivray, Maclean, Macdonald, Macdougall, with a heavy sprinkling of Campbells in powerful positions, and followed, in terms of numbers, by the other names you will find in this book. There are surprisingly many non Mac-names, such as Beaton, Black, Buchanan, Carmichael, Colquhoun, Currie, Ferguson, Graham, Lamont, Morrison, Rankin and Stewart. Many of these had their Gaelic forms, of course, but were anglicised or translated early in the kind of written records which have been consulted for this work.

In the 18th century, names were still concentrated in kinship groups in particular areas. A 'farm' did not mean one farmhouse with outbuildings and some acres of ground extending from it. A farm in 18th century Mull might have had a tacksman in its largest house, groups of smaller buildings in which unmarried farm workers lived, and, beyond that, a 'township', - a group of twenty or thirty 'huts' of stone or turf, roofed with thatch or heather, where families of subtenants lived with a cow or two of their own, ground enough for a few oats and potatoes, and holding horses and agricultural implements in common.

In such a community people married their cousins and neighbours. Children often remained with their parents until they married, except for seasonal excursions to the lowlands for harvest work. Gaelic was spoken by all, including the tacksmen, but business, such as drovers' accounting, was recorded in English.

If you should be advised in this book that your family name comes from such-and-such a farm, you may not be able to conclude that the house presently bearing the name was the residence of your forebears. For every house now surviving in Mull, ten will have stood in the past, and where a township also stood there, fifty might have borne the name. The survival of the fittest applies to houses as well as people, and the best house became the present day farm. Near modern farms, there are outhouses which were once dwellings, and there are often signs of ruins which were further dwellings. Many townships were at a distance from the main farm, which gave its name to the area. It is possible that remote communities like Inivea, above Calgary, or Tir Fhearagain, between Ardalanish and Knockvologan in the Ross of Mull, resumed life as 'summertowns' or groups of shielings where cattle were taken in summer, and that the pressure of population in the 1780s, as well as the intensified need for marketable animals, encouraged younger couples to remain on those high, west-facing hillsides. Mull people, like other highlanders, certainly preferred inland sites. Indeed, they almost seemed to have an aversion for the sea. Most of our ancestors, since these townships held the largest number of people, must perforce have come from such communities.

Problems with names and the question of clans.

This book is only concerned with Mull names as they were at the time of most of the waves of emigration, to assist the descendants of people who left in the difficult task of identifying ancestors and the places they lived in. It does not attempt to indicate which clans people belonged to. Indeed, some of the names assumed by Mull families give a quite erroneous idea of clan affiliation. In an island where, a few centuries ago, the bulk of the people were dependants or followers of clans which were obvious to their neighbours, it was unnecessary to incorporate any notion of clan in the identifying name of an individual. Instead, people were recognised by their ancestry or place of residence, so their names were compound patronymics, or nicknames showing their occupation, or names incorporating their place of residence. When more formal appellations were required in rentals of the 16th-17th centuries, patronymics were employed which strung together the forenames of the man or woman, the father, and the grandfather. There were no 'surnames' to be considered. In the 18th century the father's name might be converted into a 'surname' as Gaelic society struggled to fit into a Scots-English pattern, or the name of the protecting clan might be adopted as a surname. Occasional references in this book to surnames which existed in the 17th century only reflect conversions from Christian names, so that, except for the larger 'clan' names, most forms cannot reliably be traced back to a standard surname before the 18th century. The great variety in the spelling of Mac-names stems from the different ways the conversions were made. It would be quite wrong to assume that because the spelling of a name is different in the 18th or 19th century from the established spelling of our names in the 20th century, that we are not speaking of the same families. In the records which have supplied the information for this book, session clerks and census

5

enumerators have given their versions of both Christian names and surnames. They translated or modified what they regarded as incomprehensible Gaelic forms, and contended frequently with aliases, because surnames were still hovering between many possible styles, or people thought it more politically correct to be a McGhiel than a Macgregor. Thus we have Maclucas, becoming Macdougall, and Maceachern becoming Mackechnie. The use of an alias is not as sinister as it sounds, but only reflects the problems of presenting a name in a form recognisable to friends and strangers alike. You may be just as confounded by the multiplicity of forms in

Christian names. Marion and Sarah are variants of the same name. Ewen and Hugh are the same name. The preponderance of Biblical names, and, even more so, of names of heroes from Greek legend like Hector and Alexander, are not due to the parents' excessive Christian faith, or their constant reading of Homer's *Iliad,* but to the cultural backgrounds of the ministers baptising small Mull persons. Baptismal records were kept in English, not Gaelic, and the scribes were doing their best to translate Gaelic Christian names into forms that God, or the gods might understand. Finally, if you are principally interested in finding the place where your ancestors lived in Mull, you will find a ready answer in this book only if your name is a very localised one, such as Currie, Graham, Rose and others which are commented upon because of their clear provenance. If you are descended from Macleans, Mackinnons, or Macdonalds, the three most widely dispersed surnames, you are unlikely to be able to go straight to the family croft. Until an authoritative history of Mull is written, references to the map in this book can only point you to your most probable ancestral locations.

BEATON

One of the more illustrious of Mull names, since it was that of the family of hereditary physicians who practised at **Pennycross**, at the head of Loch Scridain in the 17th century, one of the few families to have recorded pedigrees from an earlier period. A grant of lands at Pennycross was made in 1572, and again in 1603, to a surgeon of this family, by Maclean of Duart. The Beaton medical manuscripts, in Gaelic, are preserved in the National Library of Scotland, and the Beaton pedigree is in the Laing Manuscripts in Edinburgh University Library. Malcolm Beaton, or MacBeatha, a physician, was reputed to have been on the Spanish ship, *San Juan de Sicilia,* when she was blown up in Tobermory Bay in 1588. He survived. John Beaton, born in 1594, son of Malcolm,

6

was also physician to the Macleans of Duart, and had three sons, one of whom, John, became minister of Kilninian Parish in about 1670. John was a manuscript collector and scholar. For the ins and outs of this family you should read John Bannerman's study *The Beatons*. But beware of assuming that if you have the Beaton name in your family you are descended from this group of intellectuals! Most 19th century Beatons tended to claim a relationship, understandably enough, but Dr Bannerman's scholarly hesitations in identifying descendants might give you pause. Many other Beatons in Mull provide respectable alternatives to the learned family. A strain of Beatons in **Ardalanish**, on the south coast of the Ross of Mull, remained there for several generations, and their descendants were tenants in several farms in the area, such as **Uisken, Scoor, Ardchiavaig, Ardachy, Tir Fhearagain** and **Knocknafenaig**. Beatons in **Ardtun**, in the north of the Ross of Mull also probably sprang from this branch, and went to Bruce Township in Canada about 1852. Beatons from the **Quinish** estate of the Macleans of Coll emigrated to Australia in 1852, Angus, the father being described by the Highland Emigration Society as "a fine man with [six] healthy children." Beatons spread out from the **Dervaig** area in the early 1800s, some of whom followed their probable kinsman, Angus, to Australia in 1853. Finlay Beaton from Dervaig was born about 1770 in **Sunipol** and moved to the new village of Dervaig in about 1800. A blacksmith in **Creich**, near present-day Fionnphort, Donald Beaton, gave evidence to the Highlands and Islands Commission of Enquiry in 1883, and died in Creich in 1902. James Beaton, retired master mariner in Tobermory, also gave evidence in the 1883 enquiry, as an expert on piers. The Beatons are therefore found in greatest density in the Ross of Mull, with a recorded history in **Ardalanish** in particular from the early 1700s to the 20th century. Their most typical Christian names, which give clues to their family descent, are Alexander, Angus, Neil and Roderick (Rory), and Rachel for girls, deriving from Rachel MacIntyre, born about 1765, wife of Rory Beaton, born in Ardalanish about 1760. The second greatest Beaton population density was in the rural areas around Dervaig, with considerable movement into Dervaig village when it was built in c.1800. There were six Beaton families there in the 1841 census, quite a high number for a small village.

The Mull Bells appear to have come in from other regions of Argyll, for they are numerous in the Duke of Argyll's estate census of 1779 in the mainland areas of Tullich, Drimfern and Sallachry, while there are a few in Tiree in the same year. Mull has only one cluster in the Ross, at **Ardalanish**, in 1779, consisting of Donald Bell, born about 1720, with his son Malcolm aged 30, and "their wives, daughters and maid", numbering five females. Large oaks from little acorns grow, and this small group seems to be the progenitor of some of the later Bells in Mull. An influx of Bells from Islay may have been due to Factor Mor, otherwise John Campbell of Ardmore in Islay, the hated factor of the duke of Argyll in the Ross of Mull, who brought in his favourites, and pushed out Mull tenants, claiming that the latter were lazy. It says much for the sweetness of temper of the Mull people that these favourites were not lynched, but some of them, like Ronald Bell (1820-1887) in **Deargphort**, wisely married Mull girls. Lachlan Bell, the ferryman, inn-keeper and spirit merchant at **Ulva Ferry** in the 1841 census, born c.1780, has disappeared without trace with his wife and four grown-up children by the 1851 census, but then so had most of Ulva's inhabitants in that decade! The "Christina, relict of the late John MacMillan", who is buried at Port Elgin, Ontario, was Christian Bell in Ardchiavaig before her marriage to the widowed John MacMillan in 1836, and is probably a descendant of Donald Bell in Ardalanish. Donald Bell in **Ardachy** in 1861, and born about 1820, was one of the Islay farmers brought in by the factor, like Ronald Bell, born about 1822. John Bell in **Balnahard** in the 1860s and 1870s married Elizabeth MacDiarmid from Morvern, and their son, Charles, remained in Kilfinichen parish, dying at **Bunessan** in 1942 at the comparatively youthful age of seventy-seven. Hugh Bell in Torranbeg (see present-day **Torrans**) married Mary Cameron from Ardnamurchan at the beginning of the 19th century. Mary lived on at Torrans after Hugh's death, dying there in 1857 at the age of 92. Bell women had the rather doubtful gift of longevity, for Margaret Bell, born about 1775, died in **Ardtun** aged 98 in 1873, the daughter of Malcolm Bell and Christina Macleod, and probably the granddaughter of Donald Bell in Ardalanish mentioned above. Bell descendants should concentrate on the Ardalanish forebears, or consider Islay as an alternative cradle of their family.

The name of Black, in Gaelic the Clann 'Ic Gille Dhuibh, is surprisingly current in Mull through the whole of our period, and is distributed over the island, particularly the smaller islands of **Iona, Ulva** and **Gometra.** There were Blacks in all the farming occupations, but there is a larger number of tailors, shoemakers and weavers of this name than any other. A Hugh Black, cottar in **Ardnacross**, and aged 70 in 1779, with a son of 30, may have begun the offshoot of Blacks in **Ardtun**, Ross of Mull, for the inhabitants of Ardnacross were transplanted to Ardtun in about 1791 so that the fifth duke of Argyll could practise agricultural improvements in Ardnacross. A family in **Gometra**, headed by Lachlan Black, born about 1727, seems to have fed into the Ardtun offshoot also, for they are not to be found in Gometra after 1841, although John Black was one of a group of intrepid lobster fishers on the island of **Little Colonsay**, west of Ulva, in 1851. Another Lachlan Black, who was probably a grandson of the Gometra man, settled in Ardtun after his marriage to Elizabeth Stewart in 1807. The novelist William Black (1841-1898), whose memorial lighthouse tower near Duart Castle can be seen from the Mull ferry, had no family connections with Mull. A Malcolm Black, born in Gometra about 1760, and married to Isobel Black in the 1780s, had at least nine children. His youngest son, Neil, achieved notoriety when he died in 1879 at **Kinloch** with his flesh falling off his bones. The Glasgow newspapers published the story to demonstrate the state of poverty still prevailing in

Mull. Christian names which tend to  run in Black families are Alexander, Donald, Hector, John, Lachlan, Murdoch. Girls were Ann, Catherine, Christina, Effy or Euphemia, Flora, and a curious un-Highland 'Winifred', which was an attempt to turn the Gaelic Una into English. Winifred married Donald Black in or before 1790, and lived in Ulva, where they had nine children, not quite matching the fecundity of Hugh Black and Catherine Macdonald in **Tir Fhearagain**, who had eleven between 1812 and 1836. In Torosay parish, Blacks congregated in **Kinlochspelve**. Some of them were servants to the Maclaines of Lochbuie. When Jane Maclaine of Lochbuie was preparing to move out of Moy House to make way for her new daughter-in-law in 1814, John Black was one of two faithful servants to the family of Lochbuie she could not dispense with. A John Black in the Ross of Mull, living at **Knockan** in Ardtun, was a weaver, and married Lucy Lamont in 1839. Of their eight children, the second youngest, Alexander, became minister of Portree in Skye. John died at Ardtun in 1890, aged 96. In the census of 1871, he and his wife still had five grown-up, unmarried offspring living with them in their three-roomed house at Knockan. Lucy Lamont was the daughter of Donald Lamont and Ann McNeill, and the unusual Christian name of Lucy probably came from Lucinda McNeill, wife of Archibald Campbell, tacksman of Frachadil in the 1800s. Black is said to be the oldest name in Iona, where there were ten in 1779, twenty-two in 1841, and twenty-one in 1851 after a spate of emigration. Black is notable for being a Mull and Iona name that has not died out. Its representatives can still be found in their early habitat.

A gravestone in Kilpatrick, Torosay, which is still legible today, commemorates John Buchanan, a native of that part, who executed many improvements upon the Torosay estate in the time of the late Colonel Campbell (of Possil) and departed this life in August 1848, aged 42. This John was probably related to the family of McPhananich in **Ardchoirk** in 1779, and his family name was more likely to have been McChananich, which was already Englished in **Arle** and **Ardnacross** to Buchanan. **Ardchoirk**, belonging to the duke of Argyll, and therefore a former Duart territory, was indeed a positive breeding ground of Buchanans in the 1790s and early 1800s, with a Duncan and two Neils at the top of the reproduction league. If you have Mull Buchanans in your tree, you should look first in this corner of Torosay parish. The remains of an extensive township can be seen if you take the road through Lochdon village, and bear left at Barr nam Frian, as if you were going across country to Duart Castle. In 1779 this place had eighty-three inhabitants, mostly Colquhouns and

Buchanans. As late as 1841, there were twenty-four inhabited houses, with the Buchanans reduced to six souls. A Hugh Buchanan, born about 1775, fathered a child called Archibald, who bore his father's surname, upon a Flory Fletcher of **Kinlochspelve** in 1803, but by 1808 he was respectably married to Catherine McInnes in **Fellonmore**. He reappears in the 1841 census at Kinloch with the name of Ewen, a variant of Hugh. Buchanan Christian names are drawn from a smallish pool - Duncan, Neil, Hugh, George, Alexander, Archibald and John, suggesting a small ancestral base in a single family. That family retained its home in Ardchoirk, venturing not very far afield within Mull. An Andrew Buchanan, who was a merchant in Bunessan in 1851, was born in Glasgow, but married a Mull woman in the 1840s. Although not particularly intermarried with the Mull Colquhouns, Buchanan fortunes seem to be remarkably linked with those of their fellow-countrymen, for both families remained in Ardchoirk until the second half of the 19th century, in very reduced numbers, and they must have hailed in the dim and distant past from the same part of Scotland - the east and west sides of Loch Lomond. Lachlan Maclaine of Garmony, an illegitimate son of Gillean Maclaine of Scallastle, but still a member of the island's elite, kept a diary in the 1820s in which he referred to his sister Anne Buchanan, and his brother George Buchanan. Mull people were notable for their longevity, but in 1843, during the Poor Law Enquiry, a Duncan Buchanan was said to be living in **Killean** aged 103, with his wife of 104. The 1841 census does not bear this out, giving both their ages as 85, but this might be explained by the fact that enumerators were instructed to round down the age of anyone as old as 90 !

Cameron country is traditionally in the mainland areas of south west Inverness-shire, and north mainland Argyll, but it is interesting that Blaeu's published map of Mull identifies the island as one which "lyeth ovir against Lochabir". To Timothy Pont, the minister who supplied most of the topographical information for Blaeu's map, Lochaber, home of the Camerons, was a hop, skip and jump from Mull in the days when all communications were by sea, and many Camerons must have hopped from Lochaber and Morvern to Mull in the 18th century, mainly after the Jacobite rebellion in which so many Camerons played a part. There were Camerons in Mull long before this, for in a court case in Inveraray in 1711 about herring assize duties, evidence was given by John Cameron in **Druimfin** and another John Cameron in **Achnacroish**. Hector Cameron was a tenant in **Kinloch**, at the head of Loch Scridain in 1779, and Duncan Cameron was a twenty-six-year-old merchant in **Saorphin** in the same year. Angus Cameron in **Bunessan** aged 40 in 1779, was a grasskeeper (which meant he watched that cattle didn't stray over unfenced land into neighbouring properties) with two young sons, Donald and Robert. **Knocknafenaig**, between Bunessan and Uisken, had Camerons in the 1770s whose descendants multiplied and produced three families of Camerons in this small township in the 1841 census. Most of the Knocknafenaig people left in the 1850s, and again in 1865, for Bruce County,

Ontario, where Camerons can be identified in the Port Elgin cemetery. **Uisken** and **Tir Fhearagain**, **Knockvologan** and **Iona** all had considerable families of Camerons in the 1841 census. A contingent in **Laggan**, near Lochbuie, and in **Croggan** nearby seems to have disappeared by mid-19th century. Indeed, the earlier, 18th century Mull Camerons, apart from the Ross of Mull ones, disappear from the censuses, and a new breed of Camerons comes in to take their place. **Tobermory** was not only a refuge for people evicted from Mull estates, who could not afford to go overseas, but was also, it must be remembered, a village which promised much for people evicted from Morvern, Ardnamurchan and Appin, where estates had been bought up by new landlords. Thus, with Tobermory only a ferry ride away from the mainland, a new influx of Camerons arrived in that area in the 1840s and 1850s, natives of Morvern in particular. Sometimes the men married Mull girls, but sometimes they brought wives and children with them. The Camerons who appear in the 1861 census are nearly all, once again, from the traditional Cameron homelands. Their children may have been born in Tobermory, but it is more than likely that the ancestry of the Camerons who left the north east of Mull after 1861 can only be traced back to the mainland, and not to Mull at all, except perhaps in the female line. A good example of this new phenomenon was the family of Donald Cameron, a forty-three-year-old cabinetmaker in Tobermory in 1851, with a wife called Susan. Donald had been born in Morvern, and Susan in Tobermory. They had two children, John, 13, and Dugald, 9, in the 1851 census. They applied to the Highland and Island Emigration Society to go to Australia in 1852, paid their own passage, and were described as a "good family". The place name Cameron, in the parish of Kinlochspelve, has no apparent connection with the surname.

With Argyll overflowing with Campbells, it is not surprising that it should be the fourth most common name in Mull, but it was not always thus. More than any other name, the distribution of Campbells is due to political events and to the 'planting' of Campbells in Mull. It is unlikely that there were many Campbells actually living in Mull before the 1670s, unless you count the maiden names of women who had married into the native families such as Maclean, Mackinnon, and Macdougall. In 1672, the heir to the beheaded Marquis of Argyll began to pursue his predecessor's claim to Duart lands by ejecting Maclean tacksmen, and in 1674 Aros was taken over by the Campbells. Since many Mull tacksmen were legally outlawed, they could not hang around, and within four years Argyll's men had injected Campbell tacksmen into all the former Maclean of Duart property. This does not mean that every Campbell in Mull thereafter hailed from the tacksman class. Worthy small farmers (the word crofter was not yet in use) came along with the tacksmen, and were given some land left by the 'outlaws'. Much of it was waste land - wasted by war and invasion, or simply not allocated for a number of years, and all of it was in what had now become the Argyll estates. Such was the resistance of the native families, that the Argylls, although they wished to accomplish their takeover by law alone, had to resort to invasion. This did not endear them to the inhabitants. Disaffection to the Campbells lasted for most of the 18th and 19th centuries, and many humble Campbells have taken all of that time to reinstate themselves. When the earls of Argyll were made dukes in 1701 for services to the Protestant cause, they became taken up with the things of the state, and were now just as much absentee owners as the Macleans of Duart. Even Inveraray was but a summer camp to them until Archibald, the third duke, set about restoring it. The second duke had no idea what Mull and Tiree looked like, but sat in Oxfordshire reproaching his Campbell agents for not bringing in his rents there. His demands were too much for his tacksmen, who, although not above making profits for themselves, were perhaps not altogether to blame. But many of them decided that America offered them better prospects, and left, mainly before the Jacobite rising of 1745. By this time, the worthy Campbell followers had multiplied, but had not prospered enough to go abroad. The third, fourth and fifth dukes introduced a new set of Argyllshire Campbells to collect their rents and look after their business, to make sure that the tenants were loyal to Whig government and presbyterian religion. So by the last quarter of the 18th century most Campbells were gentlemen, in that very particular Jane Austen-ish sense, trying against all the odds to remain so. Their sons went into the army with commissions, and their daughters often married other Mull names. When the fifth duke had his census made in 1779, the Ross of Mull had only one Campbell tacksman and a dozen commoners of the name, while the area extending from Aros Castle to Tobermory, had gentlemen Campbells in **Aros, Baliscate** and **Drumfin.** But respectable tenants such as Archibald, Hector, two Hughs, and John Campbell were in **Tenga** with a host of sons, **Kellan** and **Killiechronan** had Campbell tacksmen, and **Killiemor, Acharonich** and **Achadashenaig** (later **Glenaros**) established Campbell tenants. **Treshnish, Ensay** and **Sunipol** were virtually gentlemen's seats for Campbell scions, each with a sprinkling of servants and tenant farmers of the same clan. **Arin, Lagg** and **Frachadil, Penmore** and **Aird** were in the charmed circle, and even **Iona**, so particularly anti-Campbell and faithful to the old Maclean families (as Dr Johnson noticed), was well planted. **Brolass**, still not quite under Campbell power, had Maclean tacksmen, but also a few Campbell tenants. In the south east, in Torosay, only that most important of former Duart lands, **Achnacroish**, was controlled by Campbells. Sixty years later, the 1841 census of Mull shows the impact of intermarriage and economic collapse. The 'gentlemen' have largely disappeared, with their sons and daughters, although a few unmarried daughters of the old families are detectable, living in genteel poverty. How are the mighty fallen!

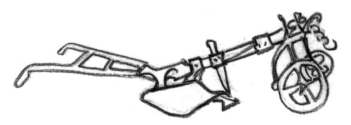

Not just these old ladies (for this was the fate of highly bred old ladies of the Maclean kind too), but the tenants seemed to slip from their positions as an elaborate game of social musical chairs was played out in Mull. In the south west, where change came about slowly, where the sixth duke's domains in the Ross were having to support more people than ever before on less produce, Campbells increased in the townships in the same way as everyone else. They were assimilated at last. Like all the other names, and in the same proportions, they were now mostly cottars and agricultural labourers, with a few tenants among them. Their minister was a Campbell, but the Rev. Donald Campbell does not seem to have been very active on their behalf, and as a result, in the 1840s, the Baptists gained a footing in the Ross of Mull. Meanwhile, in the rest of the island, Campbells had spread out from former Argyll lands, largely sold by the sixth duke to new proprietors. In 1853, Lord Strathallan's estate had Duncan Campbell, a poor widower with six children leave for Portland Bay on the *New Zealander,* described by the Highland and Island Emigration Society as "very suitable for the colony." There were so many poor Campbells that it would be impossible to name them. One outstanding one was John Campbell, born about 1832 to a tailor and crofter in **Dervaig**, Duncan Campbell, and his wife Janet Maclean. In 1892, John, aged about 60, appeared as an army pensioner at Tobermory to give evidence to the Royal Commission (Highlands and Islands,1892). The commissioners were inquiring into the clearances which had happened in Mull about fifty years earlier, being disposed to redress the balance in response to public feeling. John Campbell was an authority on every estate which had been cleared in his own lifetime. His testimony was remarkable, considering that many witnesses were unaware of who owned what, and frequently confused tenants with owners. Campbell had no such problem. He presented a fully detailed account of landownership with dates, over a period when the Keeper of Sasines himself might have had difficulty in compiling such a document. A veil had long ago been drawn over evictions from Mull, partly because at least three of the most notorious evictors had sons or grandsons who now owned the estates. Campbell, with dispassionate accuracy, and exquisite *politesse* simply stated the name of each of the guilty forebears. Of Campbell Christian names the most popular are John, Archibald, Duncan for boys, and Ann, Mary and Margaret for girls. Not an imaginative set of names - but we are speaking of a practical rather than a creative tribe. Yet certain families are enlivened by Mungo as a boy's name and Breadalbane for a girl. Many Mull people will tell you that you do not have to be introduced to a Campbell to know his surname. You can always tell a Campbell from his face. But we must regard this as a lingering piece of 17th century prejudice.

When the 5th duke of Argyll instructed that a census be taken of his Mull estate in 1779, there were Carmichaels serving the Stewarts of Achadashenaig (now called **Glenaros**), Carmichael cottars in **Baliscate,** which is now part of Tobermory, a Donald Carmichael with two sons in **Kinloch** on the shores of Loch Scridain, John Carmichael herd, at **Frachadil**, near Calgary, and a father and son at **Auchnacraig** on the way to Grass Point.

Now the duke was not the only landowner in Mull, but for some reason there are no 18th century Carmichaels on the Maclaine estates. Traditionally, Carmichaels come from the island of Lismore, which was ducal land, and this may explain a certain amount of population movement between Lismore and the duke's lands in Mull. From small beginnings the Mull Carmichaels grew - not numerically, but perhaps in importance. Duncan Carmichael who was the eleven-year-old boy living at Auchnacraig in 1779, was probably the same Duncan who married Anne Stewart about 1802, and lived in **Glennan**, Torosay. His daughter Catherine (1811-1864) married John McPhail in 1831, and they are the ancestors of many McPhails now in New Zealand. Duncan Carmichael and Anne Stewart had a son, Alexander, in 1810, brought up in Glennan, who married in 1839 a girl from the island of Luing, Mary McDougall. They lived in Bunessan where six children were born, and then moved to **Fidden**, near Fionnphort, and finally to **Beach**, where Alexander Carmichael died at the age of 50 in 1859, leaving Mary with ten children. Angus Carmichael, fifteen-year-old son of John Carmichael, grasskeeper at Achadashenaig in 1779, married Janet Campbell in 1795, and lived at **Glenaros** and **Balichtrach**. Their son Hugh (1801-1892) married Isabella McInnes and died in Tobermory. Through this line a large number of descendants have come. Another Mary Carmichael from Bunessan, born about 1815, married Donald Lamont from Duart in 1836. In 1840 they had moved to **Kinloch** where Donald was innkeeper until they went to Canada with their Lamont relations from Torosay in either 1847 or 1852, when a very large number of related Mull people, and of Lamonts in particular, settled in Grey Township. The cowherd, John Carmichael at **Frachadil**, born in 1755, married Jean McLean in 1779, and after three documented baptisms, this couple disappeared from the records. You should be warned that later 19th century Carmichaels popping up in Tobermory usually came from Ardnamurchan, and did not have a Mull background. But it does seem that, quite remarkably, a handful of Carmichaels in 1779 were the only progenitors of later Mull Carmichaels who in turn left for the colonies, and are mostly traceable. If your Mull name is Carmichael, you do not have a very onerous task in reconstructing your tree.

In the duke of Argyll's estate census of 1779, there were only four male heads of households called Clark in Mull, although it must be remembered that the duke at that time owned only a little more than half of the island, and that this group of Clarks is not therefore representative. But they might almost have been chosen to represent four parts of Mull, for they were in **Ardnacross, Kellan, Burg** and **Achnacroish** - one in each of the three parishes and another in a remote headland. They were Dugald, Donald, John and Duncan respectively, and these seem to be the main Christian names of succeeding Clarks, whether related or not. In **Iona**, a later Dugald married Mary MacFarlane in 1839. They had a daughter Helen, but disappear from Iona before the 1851 census. In **Torness** on the river Lussa in Torosay parish in 1861, a shepherd called Donald Clark with his wife Sarah and four sons, John, Donald, Alexander and

David, lived in only two rooms, but were nevertheless willing to take the local schoolmaster as a boarder. Perhaps the benefits outweighed the discomfort. Duncan Clark was in **Saorphin** in 1818 when he married Marion MacCormick, but probably died in the mid-1840s, for Marion was a widow with four children in the 1851 census of **Ardchiavaig**. The most famous Clark of all, Francis William Clark (1800-1887) was born in Elgin, and became a sheriff in Stirling in the 1820s and 1830s where he was professionally acquainted with Ranald MacDonald of Staffa, the charming and hospitable owner of the island of **Ulva**. "Staffa", as he was called, was bankrupt in 1817, and his island was later sold to Charles Macquarie. When Macquarie died in 1835, Francis William Clark bought it. With the island came about five hundred and fifty inhabitants. No census had ever been taken of Ulva although there must have been a rent roll, which would have shown tenants, but not cottars, the "supernumerary" population. Clark did make the effort to learn Gaelic to communicate with his tenantry, a promising gesture, and his first report on the island was glowing. After ten years (when the population increased still further) he decided that, as he said quite openly, he had no alternative but either to surrender his property to the crofters or to remove them. He removed them. The principal family names on Ulva were MacQuarrie and MacDonald, but apart from these, surnames in Ulva were much the same as other Mull names. The trouble is that if you cannot narrow your ancestors down to any particular place on Mull, they are just as likely to have come from Ulva, but there is no convenient passenger list to find them in. Francis William Clark is notorious as an evictor because he removed five hundred people. As one testimony states, "he was slipping them away just as fast as he could get them across the ferry." His methods were more noticeable because his estate was an island. But many other proprietors had slipped their tenants away with just as much disregard for humanity, long before Clark's evictions. Before 1850, few of them made special arrangements to send their people to Canada or elsewhere. As a result, most went to Tobermory and huddled in huts, and were lucky if the opportunity for aided emigration arose later. Seventy families were evicted from Torloisk estate in 1844, yet opprobrium does not attach to the marquis of Northampton in the way it does to Clark. One does not like to defend a man like Francis William. He may have been the bogey man of your ancestors, but at least you are unlikely, if you are a Clark, to descend from him. A humble shepherd in Torosay parish or a virtuous weaver in **Tiraghaoil** is more likely to be your progenitor, to whom you should be truly grateful for a legacy of political correctness.

The affinity between Colquhouns and Buchanans is mentioned in the Buchanan entry, as both names came originally from the Loch Lomond area, and are found in Mull in the last quarter of the 18th century in the same settlements. In 1779 a family of Colquhouns were tenants in **Tenga**, headed by Archibald, aged 36, with his three sons, Duncan 10, Angus 7, and Patrick 2. An Angus, aged 12, is the only person of this name in **Auchnacraig** in the same year, suggesting that he was either employed as a cowherd there, or being brought up by relations. But the Colquhouns' place in 1779 was principally **Ardchoirk,** north-east of Loch Don, where three mature men, John Roy Colquhoun, aged 60, Duncan Colquhoun aged 50, and Donald Colquhoun 50, were all tenants, with seven sons between them. Another John Colquhoun, aged 39, worked as a herd on the island of **Calve** in Tobermory Bay, and his son Dugald was 6. The best-known Colquhoun of this period was Robert, born about 1725, who was schoolmaster in Iona from about 1774 until 1792. We know that Robert had been a schoolmaster near Dunoon before Iona, but we do not know his own place of origin, and so cannot presume that he was related to the Colquhouns in the south east of Mull, although his age might suggest he was a brother to John Roy, Duncan and Donald. An Angus Colquhoun, born at Ardchoirk in about 1811 is still to be found there in a one-roomed house in 1861 with his Appin-born wife, Janet, son Donald, 10, son John 6. Angus junior was about to be born, and there are four daughters. These are descendants of the core families, now controlling a remarkable (for Mull) sixty acres. Another family who moved from Ardchoirk to **Ardachaoil** were Angus and Mary Colquhoun, whose son Hugh (sometimes known as Ewen) later went to **Salen** and became a lobster fisher. But by 1871 Hugh, at 75, is on the Poor Roll, and other Colquhouns in Salen have fared no better. Colquhouns in **Glencannel** in 1841 include a 74-year-old Duncan, almost certainly a relic of the Ardchoirk clan, but he is not surprisingly gone by the next (1851) census. It is very likely, if you are a descendant of Mull Colquhouns, that all roads lead back to Ardchoirk, but you will have problems with your tree in the period before the 1841 census, in making connections, since Christian names are so repetitive. The name Colquhoun itself enjoyed a certain vogue as a Christian name in the early to middle 19th century because the Maclaines of Lochbuie were, in the female line, descended from a delightfully eccentric Jacobite lawyer called Colquhoun Grant, and gave the name to one of the sons of Murdoch, 20th of Lochbuie. This Colquhoun Maclaine was born in 1828 and died in 1853 at the age of twenty-four. For a time he was the only male representative of the Lochbuies resident at Moy House, and must have inspired some of the tenants to call their sons after him.

Though some say that Currie was a name in its own right, and others that it was a corruption of McQuarrie, there is absolutely no doubt that most Mull Curries were Macvurichs, anglicised to Currie in Islay and Mull. But the same caveat applies to Curries as to Beatons. If you have Currie in your tree, and you read that it is an approximation of the Gaelic name Macvurich, and you read somewhere else that the Macvurichs were bards, or harpers, or historians to the Macdonalds, you cannot assume that your ancestors belonged to this happy breed. The Macdonalds referred to were the Lords of the Isles, and then the Clanranalds, and nobody in the Hebrides has a true pedigree dating back as far as that. Even the pedigrees of the clan chiefs, though chanted in song by their bards, cannot be put to the test, as no records exist to corroborate them. So you should try to forget the idea of being descended from the poets and historians, and simply consider it as rather an attractive idea. It is better to trust to more recent and more practical records. For instance, when Gillean Maclaine, natural son of the outrageous John Maclaine of Lochbuie, died in 1788, twenty-nine pages of accounts were prepared by his lawyers, and in them there is an entry "Donald Roy Macvurich, alias Currie." This Donald Roy is variously referred to as Donald Currie, Donald Macvurich, and Donald Roy Macvurich. He was a joiner in the 1780s. Many Curries were due to be paid out of Gillean's estate, for they seem to have been an active bunch of tradesmen, rather than small farmers, like most Mull people. Gillean had lived at Garmony as well as Scallastle, and the Curries were very concentrated in **Fishnish, Garmony, Ledirkle** and **Scallastle,** with quite a few appearing as far west as **Kinlochspelve.** Gillean Maclaine of Scallastle, who was a 'Writer' or lawyer in Edinburgh and Mull, was in charge of his father's legal affairs for a time, and tried to temper his parent's irascible behaviour with fair dealing and rational treatment. As a result, many of his Garmony Curries called their sons Gillean in his honour, and the name, along with Neil and Murdoch (another Lochbuie family name), Donald, Duncan and Hector, became a favourite Currie Christian name, to be handed down for several generations. Mull Curries did not rise to the top of the island's social pyramid, but there were intelligent schoolmasters among them. Archibald Currie, born about 1800, taught in Fishnish in the 1840s, and John Currie, schoolmaster in **Ulva** from the late 18th century until well into the 19th, helped Alexander Campbell, the editor of *Albyn's Anthology* with his collection of music in 1815. John and his wife Mary Macinnes had lived in Scallastle before moving to Ulva. A Donald Currie, house carpenter in Garmony, married Ann Buchanan, a half-sister of the illegitimate Lachlan Maclaine of Garmony, and his sons Hector and Gillean were ferrymen at the Fishnish crossing in the 1840s. Currie men married local girls from the south east corner of Mull - Macphails, Lamonts, Buchanans, Maclachlans and Blacks. A Murdoch Currie in Kinlochspelve, with his wife Sarah had nine or ten children between 1830 and 1850. Their son Donald became a schoolmaster, and their daughter Jane Jarvis was graced with yet another Maclaine of Lochbuie Christian name.

In the last quarter of the 18th century, Mull Fergusons were to be found in **Fidden**, where Duncan Ferguson, born about 1723, was the miller, with a twenty-three-year-old son, Malcolm. In **Kilfinichen**, a fifty-six-year-old John Ferguson was a mealer, as distinct from a miller, which meant he provided working horses, and generally had an investment in the farm where he paid his rent. John had a son of twenty called Hugh and a John aged twelve. In **Treshnish**, Archibald Ferguson was a ditcher, born about 1740, with sons Finlay, 12, Peter, 9, and John, 6. A very young Allan Ferguson, aged twelve was a servant in **Ardnacross** in 1779, while Alexander Ferguson, born about 1734, was in **Achnacroish** in Torosay. We cannot say whether these Fergusons were related to each other, or whether the name of Ferguson was in their case a translation of the Gaelic McFhearghuis. As with other tenants of the dukes of

Argyll, this small part of the clan may have drifted from Perthshire into mainland Argyll, and from there to Mull. By the time of the 1841 census only the Ross of Mull Fergusons have survived. Duncan Ferguson, born about 1800, was in charge of the Baptist congregation at **Bunessan** for forty-eight years, and died in 1882. He was a composer of hymns, and also had the distinction of being the first native-born Baptist in Mull. Duncan was married twice, first to Margaret Beaton in 1835, and secondly to Mary MacPherson. My own guess about his ancestry was that his father Malcolm was the son of the Duncan Ferguson recorded at **Fidden** in 1779. One of Duncan's nephews, Malcolm, or Calum Ban Ferguson, married into the Iona MacPhails, failed to have children, lost his wife in 1902, and remarried at the age of seventy a wife half his age. Also in **Iona**, an Alexander Ferguson married Isabel Black in 1821 and had eleven children, but the death register of Iona seems to groan with deceased young Fergusons from this marriage in the 1830s and 1840s. A Findlay Ferguson in **Ardtun** married Marion Black in 1809, but may not have survived after 1816. Marion, or Sarah (an alternative translation of the Gaelic Christian name) was in Ardtun in 1841 and 1851, with sons. In the north of Mull, a Neil Ferguson married Mary McLucais before 1808 and had twelve children at **Penmore**, including twin daughters, and may be the Neil Ferguson, shoemaker whose corpse lies in Calgary burial ground, under a stone engraved by his son Archibald, probably the carpenter recorded at **Aird** in the 1861 census. If you have Fergusons from Mull in your family, the chances are that you are descended from the Ross of Mull Baptist branch, or from the Penmore shoemaker.

Although the lowland Scottish name of Fletcher is associated with makers or bearers of arrows, the Fletchers of Argyll and Perthshire have come back to the English form via Gaelic. But if Mull Fletchers were MacInleisters, their name had become Fletcher in written records well before 1750. Macpherson, the translator/writer of *Ossian*, is said to have claimed that he was shown an original Gaelic manuscript by Angus Fletcher of **Glenforsa**, but the only Angus Fletcher known to have had an interest in collecting Gaelic poetry was Angus of Glenorchy, father of Archibald Fletcher, the burgh reformer. Perhaps the placename has been transmitted wrongly. In the duke of Argyll's estate census of 1779, **Glencannel,** one of the remotest valleys in Mull, and right in the centre, between Ben Talaidh and Ben More, was the home of four Fletcher families, and a group of ruins now marks the spot. One, Malcolm Fletcher, aged sixty, was a catechist, and it is hard to imagine his flock in that lonely place. But it was to remote areas that catechists were specifically directed, to make sure that the people heard the word of God where the minister could not reach them. There were Fletchers in the Lochbuie estate rentals in the 1770s and '80s - in the **Fishnish** and **Balmeanach** areas on the south east coast, "John Fletcher and his mother" sharing a possession there in 1781. It is indeed in the Craignure to Salen coastal area that we find a concentration of Fletchers. **Scallastle**, for example, was not then a single house, but had a considerable population in the river valley behind. Other Fletchers were to

be found in the two settlements known as the **Bradils,** lying between Glenforsa and Glencannel. Charles Fletcher, in Glencannel before 1750, married Catherine Fletcher, and their daughter Mary married Allan Stewart (1766-1831) of the Achadashenaig family. Neil Fletcher (b.1800), a joiner, and for a time one of a nest of Fletchers in **Penalbanach,** had the honour of having the poet Dugald Macphail as his apprentice there in 1841, but Neil moved to **Salen** village where business was no doubt brisker, before 1851. A group of Fletchers in the **Laggan** area of Kinlochspelve definitely did come from Glenorchy. Peter Fletcher, farmer of 200 acres at Laggan House in 1851, had a brother and five children who bore all the family names of Archibald Fletcher, the burgh reformer mentioned above. A Sarah Fletcher (1755-1800) married Donald MacPhail (1746-1836) so she was mother of that entrepreneurial drover family living at **Rhoail** in Glenforsa, who dominated Mull and Iona as cattle dealers long after her death. Many of their descendants are now in New Zealand. Alexander Fletcher, a shoemaker in Salen, aged seventy-three in 1883, gave valuable information to the commissioners of enquiry into the condition of the crofters and cottars in the highlands and islands about the estate of Glenforsa as he remembered it from his youth. Donald Fletcher, born about 1780, lived in the Fletcher nest of Penalbanach, near Tobermory, his wife being Catherine Patience, (probably from Ross-shire), with at least six children. Archibald Fletcher, a merchant in Tobermory in 1861, married May Borrie, daughter of David Borrie, overseer of the Torloisk estate. Altogether at mid-19th century, there were seventeen households of Fletchers in Mull, but in the Ross only a single family - that of John Fletcher, born about 1798, and his wife Marion Shaw, in **Ardtun.** They had at least six children, and John was latterly a lobster fisher. There was no doubt that the natural habitat of the Fletchers was a little woody glade on the east coast of Mull, which perhaps reminded them of their ancestral Glenorchy, home of Duncan Ban Macintyre, greatest of Gaelic poets.

GILLIES

One of the names with an astonishingly localised provenance in Mull, it appears in the area around **Penmore, Frachadil** and **Calgary** more than any other. Angus Gillies, born about 1735, married in 1768 Marion McNeill, and had five sons, John, Neil, Donald, Hugh and Alexander, and a daughter Rachel. They lived in Penmore. But a list of tenants of the extensive farm of Frachadil in 1779 includes an eighty-year-old Angus Gillies who, having been born at the end of the 17th century, demonstrates the continuing presence of the name in this corner of Mull.

Frachadil had within its bounds the hill township of **Inivea**, where Gillieses lived until Hugh MacAskill, tacksman of Talisker, in Skye, inherited Calgary House from his uncle Allan MacAskill of Mornish in 1829, and proceeded to clear the estate surrounding it. Hugh was an absentee landlord, always a bad thing for the welfare of the people, but even in his own island of Skye, Eoghainn Mor is known to have made savage clearances. The only good thing that can be said of the clearing of Inivea is that it must have been so abrupt that almost in the manner of Pompeii, the township was left to stand, its houses were not taken down, or used for other purposes, and it remains a monument to the way of life, in the first quarter of the 19th century, of three or four families of Gillieses. Another concentrated showing of Gillieses was at **Reudle**, on the way from Calgary to Kilninian kirk. Here an Alexander Gillies and his wife Christina Beaton had at least eleven children between 1802 and 1827, while a Donald and his wife Margaret MacLean had six over the same years, and an Angus and his wife Marion MacLucais, beginning five years later, had eight. All three families lived in Reudle, and all three had an Angus, a Donald and a John, showing that one cannot escape duplication of names, but must tread warily and choose one's ancestors with care. James is a less likely Gillies name, but a James who was gardener at both Torloisk and Moy was treasured by his employers. "I hope", wrote Jane MacLaine of Lochbuie to her son Murdoch in 1814, "that you find him as reasonable and discreet a servant as your dear Father and I have found him." One or two Gillieses surfaced dangerously on Ulva around the time that the proprietor, Francis William Clark was beginning to think he would be better off with an empty island - that is, in the 1840s. One such was Alexander Gillies, born about 1814, a tenant in **Ormaig**, a township on the west side of Ulva which can still be seen in a two hour walk from the Ulva ferry. Alexander (who was almost certainly from one of the three Reudle families) married Mary MacDonald in the island of **Little Colonsay** in 1842, and leaping out of the way of the Clark evictions, took up lobster fishing on Little Colonsay. He soon had to contend with his mother-in-law, Catherine Rankin living with them, but as she was a midwife, she was a welcome addition. As the widow of a Little Colonsay man, she may even have given her son-in-law shelter there. Alexander and Mary were still on Little Colonsay in 1861, having added the statutory Angus to their offspring. A Lachlan Gillies in Tobermory after 1840 has to be treated with care, for he was originally from Ardnamurchan, not Mull. Some Gillies girls' names make them sound like a frieze of goddesses - Barbara, Emilia, Flora, Grace and Rachel. There were no Gillieses, to my knowledge, in the Ross of Mull.

Grahams are an ancestor-hunter's dream, as they appear first in Mull in three beautifully demarcated places, and when some of them did disappear, they went to a defined part of Canada, where many of their descendants are still living. In fact some of their descendants are still in the island of Mull itself, which is not always the case with Mull names. In the duke of Argyll's census of his estate in 1779 we find Grahams in **Ardnacross, Achnacroish** and **Bunessan**. Now we do know that the fifth

Duke moved Ardnacross tenants to Ardtun in the Ross of Mull in 1791, so that Alexander Graham, born about 1747, his wife, Effie MacKiechan and their two small sons John and Angus were probably parties in this manoeuvre. Angus was to marry Catherine MacKinnon in 1814, and lived in **Ardtun** until his death in 1858, providing a rare documented piece of continuity in a period when it was usually impossible to bridge the gap from 1779 to 1841. In **Achnacroish**, Torosay parish, Donald Graham's descendants are not so easy to trace, and a 1793 rental of Duart, the duke's part of Torosay, shows only a Duncan Graham as tenant in **Kilpatrick.** However, the 1779 presence in Bunessan of an Angus Graham aged 84 provides us with the name of the patriarch of the Bunessan branch, who were millers operating from the mill which is still visible as a ruin as you swing down into the village today. Angus was the miller, his son Duncan (born c.1735) followed him, but in the 1841 census, no Graham is listed in Bunessan, and no other miller is mentioned. Meanwhile, in 1841, the Grahams were to be found half a mile along the road in Ardtun where four separate households headed by Duncan Graham, 45, Angus Graham, 60, Margaret Graham, 50, and Angus Graham, 60, had a score of descendants living with them. (Ages in the 1841 census were rounded down to the next factor of five). Margaret was the widow of John Graham, schoolmaster in Bunessan. They had married in

1816. Margaret died in 1876 aged 92, so it is very possible that her husband John was the small boy, born in 1776, who had come from Ardnacross to Ardtun, for the second Angus Graham above was her brother-in-law, the Angus who had married Catherine MacKinnon. If all this is beginning to sound like the book of Genesis, you should bear with me, for I am approaching Duncan Graham, farmer, Inspector of the Poor, lover of several women and father of several natural children before he married Flora MacArthur in 1839. In Mull, when a man became "a bit of a lad", he seemed to throw himself into the role, and I can name about six who were well known sinners in the 1830s. Before this, the ministers seemed to have had a tight rein. Duncan's natural children were taken on, happily or unhappily, by his Tiree wife. His qualifications for Inspector of the Poor in the Ross did not seem to be compromised by his peccadilloes, and his legitimate son, Forbes Graham, carried on the tradition by having an illegitimate son Archibald born in 1871. A number of Grahams, not necessarily closely connected with Duncan, but certainly related, sailed from Tobermory about 1842 to settle in a place called Bunessan in Glenelg Township, Ontario. Grahams who remained in Mull married MacEacherns, MacMasters, MacLachlans and MacLeods, so that these names should be scrutinised carefully in the compiling of a Graham tree. The few Grahams who materialised in **Tobermory** after 1850 include James Graham, postmaster there.

But the prize for endurance should go to Donald Graham, shepherd in the loneliest spot in Mull, in the parish of Kinlochspelve, **Glenlibidil**, who, with his Perthshire-born wife Ann and five children aged 10, 8, 6, 4, and 2, appear in the 1861 census. Mothers of today who claim they have cabin fever should be grateful that they did not live there. Donald Whyte, expert on Scottish surnames, suggests that Graham was a MacGregor alias.

In Mull, Hendersons appear in surprising numbers in **Tobermory** in 19th century censuses, but this influx, when investigated, appears to date from the expulsion of small cottars and crofters from Ardnamurchan by Sir James Riddell in 1828. There were some Hendersons in **Glencannel** in Mull in the ducal census of 1779, headed by Angus, 34. Unfortunately his three sons were not named by the enumerator, and a Duncan Henderson, 80, living nearby, is not identified as a relation, but simply as "a poor man". A large number of Hendersons in Tiree in the 18th century may account for some descendants in Mull, as there was always a certain amount of intermarriage within the Argyll estates of Tiree and the Ross of Mull. Henderson would seem to be an English form of the earlier McEnrick. John Henderson or McEnrick in **Treshnish** married Janet Campbell before the registers for the parish of Kilninian began in 1766, and it is my theory that a Duncan Henderson in Treshnish who had had three natural children by three different mothers between 1795 and 1796, and then married the girl next door, Mary McInnes, in 1806, was their son. Duncan and Mary went on to have seven legitimate children between 1806 and 1821 - Janet, Mary, Donald, Julian (girl), Catherine, Angus and Alexander. Mary reappears as a widow aged 60 in the 1841 census of **Ensay**.

This is one of those families sometimes referred to as a binomial, or double-named sept, like MacDougall/MacLucas. The Gaelic form in Argyll and Invernessshire was MacUalrig or MacCualrig, but does not appear at all in that version in Mull, while the adjacent island of Tiree had many of that name in the ducal census of 1779. There is a story that one of the Cassilis Kennedys, called Ulrick, had to flee from Ayrshire to Lochaber in the 15th century, where he became the eponymous head of a new sept, MacUlrick or MacUalrig. From there his descendants spread to the islands. If this was the case, he certainly had a numerous progeny in Tiree. The only Kennedys in the duke of Argyll's lands in Mull in 1779 were Allan and Duncan in **Frachadil**. The estates of the MacLaines of Lochbuie do not show MacUalrigs or Kennedys in the 18th century. It is not difficult to make the connection between thirty-six Kennedys in the eastern parishes of Torosay and Kilninian in 1841 and Ulrick's supposed descendants, but two or three Kennedy families in the Ross of Mull at the same time would have come via Tiree. By 1851 the total number of Kennedys is only slightly greater, but by the 1861 census there is a marked increase in Tobermory. This suggests to me that most 19th century Kennedys in Mull were later arrivals from the mainland.

LAMONT

Although Lamonts came originally from Cowal, they were settled in Mull by the middle of the 18th century in Torosay Parish, in the area once belonging to the Macleans of Duart, and taken over by the Campbells of Argyll. Their presence in 1779 in **Treshnish** as servants to Campbell tacksmen there, and Lamont tenancies in **Iona** at the same time, suggest loyalty to the dukes. But Tiree, wholly possessed by the duke of Argyll in the later 18th century, was so full of Lamonts, that it is arguable that Mull Lamonts moved from Tiree rather than from mainland Argyll. In **Achnacroish** lands, in Torosay, where there were Campbell factors, an extended family of Lamonts, headed by the schoolmaster of Lochdonhead, Allan Lamont, and his wife Mary MacDougall, who lived at **Gorten**, were people of considerable talent and education who were active in the church and in the enumeration of the first two official censuses of Torosay. A letter survives today from Allan Lamont to his son-in-law Angus MacPhail in Iona, describing conditions in Gray County, Ontario after he and no fewer than forty relations had emigrated in about 1852. Letters from emigrants were eagerly welcomed by everyone left behind, who might still be considering going to Canada. They were written in English, not Gaelic, and Allan speaks of meadows and orchards and warmth unknown in the "old country". Referring to his life in Mull, he says, "I regret very much that I have spent most of my days under so many masters - landlords, Writers (that is, lawyers), chamberlains, factors, etc., and would require to be as humble to every one of them as a mouse under the cat's paw". Allan's relations included Donald Lamont, the innkeeper of Kinloch and his wife Mary Carmichael. A large number of descendants of this remarkable family are now in Monkton, Ontario. **Ulva** and **Gometra** contained many Lamonts who moved to the Ross of Mull and Iona with changes of proprietors, and resulting evictions. The well-known "character", poet and songwriter, Angus Lamont, (1771-1856), son of Donald Lamont and Effy Black in Ulva, was official guide to the antiquities of Iona from 1840, and although he did not himself have a large family, there must be many descendants of his parents around the world, as well as in Scotland. A lateral relation was Alexander Lamont of **Bearnus** in Ulva, who married Mary Lamont in 1778. Another Ulva Lamont, Archibald, who married Mary McIntaylor, or Taylor, had at least six children, and yet another Archibald in **Soriby**, Ulva, married to Margaret Lamont had eleven! A third Archibald betook himself to **Taoslin**, near Bunessan. An Allan Lamont from **Oskamull**, Kilninian Parish, who married Jean McLean, had seven children, and emigrated from Oskamull, on Lord Strathallan's estate on the ship *New Zealander* to Portland Bay in 1853, was described as heading "a poor family, daughters strong and healthy, but boys appear to have wanted food". All in all, the Lamonts were poor, but talented and intelligent, like the family from Torosay, who, having crossed the Atlantic safely, saw their father Duncan die between Lachine and Kingston, on the last lap. They settled in Caledon and Saugeen, in Ontario. It is to be hoped that all these Lamonts overseas have not succumbed to pronouncing their name LaMONT, with the emphasis on the last syllable, when it is of course on the first, like a certain British Chancellor of the Exchequer, whose ancestors, we are glad to say, did not come from Mull, but from Bute. His bland acceptance of this mispronunciation is said to have contributed to the downfall of the Conservative party in Scotland.

Everyone knows that David Livingstone, the great missionary and explorer, came from Ulva stock, and anyone I have ever spoken to with Mull Livingstones in their tree, has claimed David's father and grandfather, both Neils, as far-out relations. Because of the David Livingstone connection, there is a notion around that Livingstone is an Ulva name, but in fact David's grandfather, Neil Livingstone, came from **Lettermore** on the east side of Loch Frisa, and married Mary Morrison from Lettermore in 1774. They moved around 1780 to Cove in **Ulva**, and then to **Ferininardry** where David's father Neil was baptised in 1788. The Livingstones are very evenly dispersed in Mull as early as the ducal census of 1779, when they are found in **Creich, Shiaba** and **Ardtun** in the Ross of Mull, and in **Aros, Druimfin,** Achadashenaig (now called **Glenaros**) in the east. There are some in **Sunipol, Arin, Ardchoirk** and **Achnacroish.** Of these 18th century people, perhaps the most interesting are Duffice Livingstone in Arin and Duslea Livingstone in Ardchoirk, if only for their Christian names. In the sixty years between the 1779 census and the 1841 one, Livingstones appear to have remained in this geographical formation, but with a slight weighting in the curiously shaped part of Kinlochspelve parish known as Ton-tyr on Blaeu's map, which includes **Croggan, Drimnatain** and **Dalnaha.** Angus Livingstone and his wife Marion (or Sally, or Sarah) MacFadyen in Drimnatain had at least nine children between 1797 and 1816, and one of their sons, Gilbert, born in 1799, was a tenant in Dalnaha in 1841 and 1861, with a wife named Julian. Julian was a name which ran in one of the branches of the Maclaines of Lochbuie. As late as 1871, the road from Barachandroman to Portfield still held the largest concentration of Livingstones, with eleven families of the name. A farm called Castle Roy, no longer to be found on the ordnance survey map, with four separate households, had Alexander, Neil, David and Angus as heads of families in 1871. A Duncan Livingstone in Croggan had nine children between 1802 and 1818. In the Ross of Mull, another Duncan married into the Ardachy MacCormicks in 1811, had at least nine children, and died at **Kintra** in 1847. A later and distinguished member of the family was the poet Duncan Livingstone (Donnchadh MacdhunShleibhe), born in 1877 at **Reudle**, near Torloisk. He settled in South Africa in 1903 and began rather late in life to write Gaelic poetry and essays. Other Livingstones were Donald, born about 1775 who began life in Shiaba and ended in Ardtun, John in **Penmore** who married Catherine Campbell in 1805 and had thirteen children, John in **Tobermory** who married Ann MacDougall in 1808 and had six. If you have Livingstone connections dating back to as recent a period as the 1890s, it is most likely that you stem from the Dalnaha families. You will be interested

24

to read, in the Royal Commission, Highland and Islands *Minutes of Evidence II, Vol.XXXIX, part 1, 1895*, several pleas for land from Dalnaha Livingstones such as Allan, aged 25 in 1894, Duncan aged 35, and John aged 31. Of the three, only Allan was competent to answer questions in English, and the other two had their Gaelic answers interpreted. This does not mean that they had no English, but simply that an interpreter was offered, and that they felt more comfortable in their own language. The enquiry had been set up to discuss the possibility of restoring land which once had been arable, but was now part of sporting estates, to members of the native population. All the Livingstones cast covetous eyes upon the lands of Laggan, further down towards Lochbuy. What they actually gained from their petitions is a story beyond the scope of this book.

Coming top of the second league of Mull names in frequency of occurrence, although not found in its present day form in 17th century rental lists, the name Macarthur appears to have multiplied in the last quarter of the 18th century and the first quarter of the 19th. Writers on Scottish surnames seem to agree that they were a branch of the Clan Campbell, so that one would expect them to be prominent in the lands taken over by the dukes of Argyll from the Macleans of Duart. In the duke of Argyll's census of these lands, taken in 1779, the majority of Macarthurs are to be found scattered over the farming townships of the Ross of Mull, in **Ardchiavaig, Tir Fhearagain, Knockvologan, Fidden, Pottie, Creich, Suie** and **Assapol. Iona** also had three tenant farmers with their families in 1779. Only one significant family of Macarthurs appears in Kilninian parish at this time, in **Inivea**, where Neil Macarthur married Mary Macneill in 1767, and where their children, Margaret, Archibald, John, Malcolm, twins Florence and Marion, John and Roderick were baptised between 1768 and 1779. Later, in Kilninian parish, in 1824, the marriage of Peter Macarthur of **Ardura** to Miss Flora Maclean of **Kengharair** was important enough to be reported in the *Edinburgh Annual Register.* The most colourful Peter Macarthur in Mull was undoubtedly the son of John Macarthur in Uisken and his wife Catherine Campbell, who went to Iona, where Peter (the gold) was born in 1816. His story is told by E. Mairi Macarthur in her book, *Iona.* This Peter and his wife, were, like many others of their extended family, buried in Lovat cemetery, Ontario. We do not have names of the 18th century inhabitants of **Ulva**, but it is likely that there was a large number of Macarthurs, one of them being the famous Archibald, piper to Ranald Macdonald of Staffa, supposed to have been taught by MacCrimmon of Skye. Archibald married Janet Weir in 1801, and had at least six children. He is the subject if a caricature by John Kay in *Kay's Original Portraits.* He piped on the occasion of the visit of George IV to Edinburgh in 1822, and died about 1834, having been allowed to stay on in Ulva after that island was sold to Charles Macquarie. Although Macarthurs were prolific, most did not have quite as many children as Donald in **Burg** (Kilninian parish) who with his wife Mary Macdonald whom he married in 1785, had eight sons and three daughters before 1805. Another Donald in **Ardalanish** married Mary McKinnon in **Shiaba** in 1823 and had an Annabella to distinguish their offspring from others. They later lived in Glenelg Township in Ontario. But if you are descended from a Dugald married to a Mary Macarthur, you must take care, since two couples with exactly the same names married in the same year, and the two Dugalds died in 1859. You will need a great deal of detective work as well as some family information to unravel these two families. Where a detective would have been really useful would have been in the strange story of the death of Duncan Macarthur, **Knockvologan**'s wife, Margaret Morrison, in 1848. Duncan and Margaret had been married on 8 December 1847. A child, Mary, was born to them on 14 January 1848. But on 19 June 1848, the session clerk entered the death of Margaret in the death register, for which Iona parish is distinguished, in the following cryptic manner. "Margaret Morrison, wife of Duncan Macarthur Knockvologan is supposed to die suddenly with the cramp and one of the masons at the North Bay is a corpse this day of the same disease, both having been at their ordinary work the evening preceding their death". I do not imply anything here, and do not wish the Macarthurs to rise indignantly in Duncan's defence, but how easy it must have been to get away with murder in Mull in 1848!

Small pockets of MacCallums are dotted about Mull in 18th century records. They are in **Ardnacross, Treshnish, Fidden, Iona** and **Kilpatrick** in Torosay. The Treshnish MacCallums, Duncan, and his wife Janet Campbell, who married in 1773, may have been responsible for a proliferation of the family in **Calgary** and **Ensay,** for they had at least seven children. The small and beautiful hamlet of **Haunn,** part of the Treshnish estate, was also a MacCallum nest. Another Duncan MacCallum who married Mary MacMillan in 1773 came from Calgary, and his son John, born in 1782 moved to **Ardtun** in the very early 1800s, married Mary MacLean, and founded a Ross of Mull branch which is still represented in **Ardfenaig** today. MacCallums were fishermen in **Kintra** in the mid-19th century. The MacCallums were also millers in various parts of Mull. Lachlan MacCallum was the miller at **Torloisk** at the time of his marriage to Mary MacKinnon in 1778, and was afterwards miller on **Ulva.** They had eight children including Charles, who went on living in **Cragaig of Ulva** until around 1828, but disappeared from sight after that. Hugh MacCallum, in **Knock** in 1861, moved to Morvern to be miller at Savary. John MacCallum was miller in **Bunessan** in the early 1800s. A John MacCallum in **Duart** in the 1841 and 1851 censuses married Anne MacLachlan from Morvern and had his wife's hundred-year-old father living with them in 1851. Their son Andrew was assisted by the Highland and Island Emigration Society to emigrate to Portland Bay in 1854 with his wife Mary and infant Lachlan, the latter dutifully named for the venerable grandfather. One of the most able MacCallums in Mull was the **Tobermory** solicitor John MacCallum, the son of a Tobermory crofter, who was born about 1821 and gave evidence to the

Napier Commission when they were enquiring into the condition of crofters and cottars in 1883. John MacCallum was a voluble man, who at the age of sixty-two could still irritate the commissioners by his rebellious attitudes, his socialist principles and his defence of powerless crofters. In his fourteen pages of evidence, published in 1884, he described the gradual loss of crofting land in the vicinity of Tobermory, naming the saints and sinners concerned in a manner which could hardly be called impartial. Without this testimony, we might be led to believe that certain Mull crofters accepted their fate of eviction with resignation, unlike the militant crofters of Skye. But the truth seems to be that Mull evictions never hit the headlines in the newspapers of the day. John MacCallum gave much of his time, in these days before Legal Aid, to writing letters on behalf of illiterate underdogs in their endless disputes with landlords. Neil MacCallum, a boatman in **Creich**, and his wife Mary MacLean win the MacCallum prize for fecundity with their family of ten children born between 1832 and 1850. Like many other Mull families, however, they were fortunate in having a grandmother, Marion Maclean, nearby, who took some of the children under her wing at **Deargphort.**

In the middle of the 19th century MacColl was only about the twentieth most common name in Mull, but its traditional associations with the name Macdonald may have something to do with this balance. I say associations because no one knows just what the connection is. Clann Cholla were the children of Coll, and there were many Macdonalds with the Christian name of Coll. Macdonald was the most common name in Mull after Maclean, yet in the duke of Argyll's census of 1779 there were only about seven or eight MacColl families scattered around the island, and a few single men working as unmarried servants. John MacColl in **Baliscate,** Tobermory, born about 1734, had four sons, John, 13, Archibald, 8, Duncan, 4, and Hugh 1. Duncan MacColl in **Killiemor** had Hugh, 10, John, 8, Duncan, 3 and an infant Samuel. In the farm of Achadashenaig there was a grandfather Duncan, 71, his son Hugh, 35, and his son Duncan, 3. So monotonous are the names of the MacColls that it was a relief to find a stone in the kirkyard of Kilninian, erected by Lord Alwyne Compton of **Torloisk** to the memory of Angus MacColl, carpenter there, who died on 27 October 1906 aged 71. An Archibald MacColl aged 53 was an auctioneer in **Tobermory** in the 1861 census, with seven children. He probably auctioned livestock and agricultural implements. A Charles MacColl, in Tobermory in 1851 as a schoolmaster aged 34, was married to Hester Campbell. A Donald MacColl and his wife Mary Stewart lived in **Gometra** in the early 1800s, were later tenants in Tobermory, and are buried in Knock. On their gravestone, some of their children are named as John, Solomon, Janet and David. Dugald MacColl (1788-1863) of Iona village originally came from **Corkamull**, son of Neil MacColl and Catherine Campbell, married Flora MacInnes in 1815, and lived in **Iona** until 1863, when he died a pauper, which, in those days, simply meant that he was on the Poor Roll. Duncan MacColl (1810-1882) was a

27

surgeon who in various censuses features in the houses of the gentry where he appears to have been acting as a private practitioner. Dr Hector MacColl (1799-1891) was another surgeon, this time mainly in Tobermory where he practised for fifty years. In the Ross of Mull, a John MacColl (c.1800-1874), a cottar in **Fidden** married Euphan MacPhail in 1846 and had four children, Hugh, John, Anne and Robert, Robert in turn (in 1876) marrying a girl from Fidden, Mary McNiven. Altogether, the Mull MacColls of the 18th and 19th centuries were not an exciting clan, the most characterful being the doctor, Hector, who remained a bachelor, and is therefore not of excessive interest to ancestor hunters.

A Ross of Mull family of great local distinction - "local" meaning within Scotland, where their present-day descendants are Scottish Nationalists. The name was also rendered as Maccarmaig, and may have been exported with that spelling. Donald Maccarmaig in **Saorphin**, near Loch Assapol was a tenant there in 1779, aged 45, with four sons, Dugald, Sandy, James and Duncan. At **Suie**, Neil, born about 1729 had an eleven-year-old son Hugh, while Murdoch, at 78 had grandsons Dugald, Murdoch and John. Another John, an old man of 90, is listed at the end of the Suie names in patriarchal solitude. In **Ardtun,** Donald Maccarmaig the miller is 57, with a twelve-year-old son, Allan. Thus we have the triangular base of the Maccormick family, set one mile apart, and ready, in the last quarter of the 18th century, to spread out over the Ross and **Iona.** Sandy Saorphin married Ann Bell, and moved to Ardtun. Allan Ardtun married Ann Morison, and became a tenant in **Shiaba.** The race of Maccormicks flourished and multiplied principally in the settlement behind the present-day farm of Saorphin and in **Ardachy.** Every branch had a John, and it was the Johns who made the name memorable - John the merchant in **Kintra,** John the schoolmaster in **Catchean,** John the schoolmaster in **Creich,** with his eleven children, John the shoemaker in **Iona,** John the quarrier at Creich, John the journalist and writer of books on Mull, and, eventually, John Macdonald Maccormick founder of the National Party of Scotland. Present-day Maccormicks are well aware of their roots, being a well-organised, active clan. They hold reunions and make speeches, being politicians at heart. Perhaps their family activist, John in Catchean, started them on that track when he gave evidence to the Highlands and Islands Commission in 1883, at the age of 55, identifying the problems of his fellow crofters as due entirely to high rents and bad pasturage. But for sheer mellow fruitfulness, the Maccormick crown must go to the SSPCK schoolmaster, John, who lived from 1784 to 1879. He married in 1819, Mary Macdonald of **Tiraghaoil,** halfway between Bunessan and Fionnphort, daughter of Coll Macdonald and Janet Maccormick. When John and Mary reached the ages of 64 and 56 respectively their grown up children were still with them, as is the manner of Mull families. The schoolhouse had four rooms, a palace compared with their neighbours' humble abodes, but with seven children at home, daughter Janet, 25, son

Dugald, 23, and son Coll, 19, were farmed out to Janet Maccormick, their grandmother at Tormore. So it was in many a Mull family in the mid-19th century. When we think a grown child has flown the nest, we only have to look next door to find him, with a grandparent, an uncle or an aunt. Later branches of Maccormicks had their own private burial ground at **Achaban,** overlooking Loch Potie, which puts them on a level with the Maclaines of Lochbuie in the grandeur stakes.

If genealogy were simple, we might venture to say that all the Macdonalds in Mull (and it is the next most common name after Maclean) started out as followers of the Lords of the Isles, who were Macdonalds, and stayed on after the Macdonalds gave way to the Macleans and the Macleans gave way to the Campbells. There is possibly a modicum of truth in this premise, but the fact is that when patronymics were replaced by surnames in the 17th-18th century, many people adopted the name of Macdonald as the nearest approximation to their ineffable singular names. This only goes to underline the fact that you cannot really formulate a tree that goes back before 1700 unless you have the good fortune to belong to a family whose ancestors were enumerated in some privately owned document. I know of no such documents relating to Mull Macdonalds. The heaviest concentration of Macdonalds in the early 19th century was in the smaller islands - **Ulva,** where, in the 1841 census, nearly 25% of all persons were Macdonalds, **Little Colonsay** and **Gometra** combined, where over 50% of all individuals were Macdonalds, and the island of Iona with 20% of the population Macdonalds. In the parish of **Kilfinichen** and **Kilvickeon,** I like to think of John Macdonald, born about 1734, and living in Saorphin, with his sons Hugh, 9, John, 7, Sandy, 5, and James, 3, in 1779, as the ancestors of many Ross of Mull Macdonalds. There were many schoolmasters of the name, notably John who was the parish teacher in **Bunessan.** He was born in **Tobermory** in about 1799, and married a girl called Marion Macdonald about 1830. Their children, Dugald, Margaret, Alexander, John Duncan, Angus, Betsy, Ann, Georgina, Mary and Hester, were all born in Kilfinichen parish between 1831 and 1853, and their house, with the princely number of seven rooms, must have been one of the very few in the parish suited to a large family. However, John had a namesake who was the parochial schoolmaster at **Tiroran,** on Loch Scridain, born about 1819, and married to Christina Aitchison, who must not be confused with him. He had just as many children, - Donald, Mary, Sally, William, Jessie, John, Jane, Ann, Archibald and Mary and was schoolmaster in **Carsaig** in the 1871 census. Yet another schoolmaster, Donald Macdonald taught at **Killunaig,** and married Elizabeth Macintyre in 1826, but became a tenant farmer in Ardachy, and later at **Lee.** Their children were Euphemia, Isabella, Charles, Susan, Margaret, Robina, Robert, Neil and Peter. As the Christian name most used for Macdonald male children was John, I cannot help but select another for special comment - John Macdonald, precentor in Iona, who married Marion MacPhail of the **Iona** cattle dealer family in **Culbuirg,** in 1851.

MULL
PLACENAMES
MENTIONED
IN THE TEXT

John was the son of the Iona boat-builder Donald Macdonald, and Catherine MacGilvray. In 1852 a large group of Macphails and Macdonalds left Iona and sailed on the *Marmion* for Australia. John's wife Marion must have died in Australia when he was prospering there, for he returned to Scotland in 1871 to marry her sister-in-law, my own widowed great great grandmother, Sally Lamont, when he was described grandly as a "landed proprietor". Some Macdonalds from Ulva and Gometra managed to survive the evictions of the 1840s because they were lobster fishers, and therefore contributing to the economy, as did Joseph Macdonald, innkeeper on Ulva, whose family had been in charge of the inn (now The Boathouse, and still dispensing homemade soups and cakes) since the days of Ranald Macdonald of Staffa. If you are looking for your Macdonalds in Mull, and are sadly disappointed by this skimming of the surface, I can only assure you that it would take a book of a thousand pages to treat this name in a satisfactory manner.

Clann 'Ic Dhughaill is one of the four earliest clans of Mull, for the MacDougalls of Lorn held Mull in the late 13th century, and if we can assume that their followers were the ancestors of later MacDougalls, we might say that MacDougalls had a greater antiquity than even Macleans and Macdonalds in the island. It was this clan that built the chain of castles overlooking and guarding the Sound of Mull at Ardtornish, Aros and Duart. In the 18th century there were fewer MacDougalls in the Ross of Mull area than anywhere else. If there was any concentration of the clan, it was in the lands around Duart Castle like **Kilpatrick** (Torosay) and in the coastal strip near **Fishnish**. It was as if the descendants of the great clan wished to be as near the heartland of Lorn as they could be. If your search for MacDougall ancestors has come to a standstill, you should consider the name MacLucas (see separate entry) as a variant, for in Mull particularly, MacLucases were given to becoming MacDougalls during the time of the Englishing of surnames. The old parish register of Kilfinichen and Kilvickeon records a marriage on 2nd February 1813 of "Neil McDonald in Siaba and Mary McLucais in Torranuachdrach". The bride is the well-known authoress of the hymn *Child in the Manger*, and in the baptism entries for her first eight children, the style is the same Neil McDonald and Mary McLucais their lawful daughter Flora, etc. But the ninth child, baptised in 1831 at **Shiaba**, is Jean daughter of "Neil McDonald and Mary McDougall", and the tenth child, Coll, has the same mother's name. Other MacLucases seem to have suffered the same fate, but we shall never know if they expressed any preference for MacDougall or had it thrust upon them. Mary MacDonald or MacLucas or MacDougall, was a sister of Duncan MacDougall, a prime mover in the establishment of the Baptist church in Tiree.

In the 1851 census there were sixteen households in Mull in which the main surname was MacLucas, and in 1861 eleven, a remarkable survival considering the scale of emigration in the 1850s. It is possible that the younger generation liked to change their names just as much as they liked to emigrate, while older people staying behind stuck to MacLucas. In the 1851 census of Mull, MacDougall was the ninth most common name. In **Ardachy**, Allan MacDougall, born about 1800, was married to Ann MacGillivray, with three daughters, Isabella, Annabella and Catherine. Allan died some time in the 1850s, and his widow and daughters are in the 1861 census of **Bunessan**, but not there in 1871. Elizabeth MacDougall, a spirit dealer and widow in **Tobermory** in 1851 had a nineteen-year-old daughter Ann, schoolmistress in Tobermory, while in the same census, Eliza MacDougall was teaching in Portmore, Tobermory and Isabella MacDougall was conducting a school of industry for girls in **Dervaig** - early examples, for Mull, of female teachers. Coll MacDougall was a blacksmith in **Ulva** in the 1770s. Dugald MacDougall, born in 1753 married Effy MacNaughton in 1776 and lived at **Lettermore**, where at least six children were baptised. Another Dugald in Ulva married Mary Black in 1797, but they and their eight children may have seen the writing on the wall when Ranald MacDonald, their proprietor, went bankrupt about 1817. Before surveyors were very common in Mull (the landowners usually brought them in from elsewhere) John MacDougall was surveying in Tobermory in the early 1800s and married his namesake Margaret MacDougall. Twin boys, not uncommon in MacDougall families, were born to them in 1814 and baptised Donald and Dugald. Other MacDougalls are discoursed upon in the MacLucas entry.

In 1912, *The Oban Times* ran a series of articles on surnames which included the name MacKechnie. It was asserted that MacKechnie and MacEachern were the same name, but within a week or so an irate J.M.Mackechnie wrote in to say that it was quite wrong to suggest that MacKechnie was the English form of MacEachern, and misleading to pronounce that all MacKechnies were therefore MacEacherns originally. This objection might hold water as far as Kintyre and Islay MacKechnies are concerned. I can only say that there were no MacKechnies in Mull records before 1840, and my own great great grandfather, John MacEachern (1811-1882) was born a MacEachern and died a MacKechnie. His son Donald MacEachern (1845-1923) fluctuated between the two forms, but as a published Gaelic poet he retained his Gaelic name, Domh'ull Ban Mac Iain 'ic Eoghain. This is a clear case of MacKechnie being used as an English 'translation' of MacEachern, when the latter name, more euphonic to my ear at least, might easily have been retained. Those who left Mull for Canada and Australia before the second half of the 19th century have been fortunate enough to be able to keep the purer version of the name, and there are still MacEacherns in many Scottish telephone directories, showing that it was not regarded by everyone as the unassimilable name of a Celtic savage. For changes in surnames often occurred following an incident in which the owner of an 'outlandish' surname was supposedly embarrassed by his highland name in a lowland environment, and clutched at some similar sounding name which had apparently been found acceptable. This arbitrary adoption of surnames was not confined to MacEacherns, but muddies the waters of nomenclature everywhere. J.M. MacKechnie may have been correct in asserting that MacEacherns and MacKechnies were two separate families, but no one had prevented one passing into the other's camp for the flimsiest of reasons. The earliest references I have found to Mull MacEacherns shows them on Mackinnon land in Mishnish. In a court case in Inveraray in 1711, Kenneth MacEachern and Eachern MacEachern in **Penalbanach** were standing up for their laird, John Mackinnon of Mishnish in a confrontation in the change house (pub) in Tobermory when they told John Campbell, collector of excise duties, that they would tramp his face in the midden. It was rather dangerous to threaten a Campbell in these terms, as juries at Inveraray tended to be made up entirely of Campbells, but the MacEacherns got off lightly with a £10 fine. Their presumed descendants remained in the Ardmore area for at least another century (Penalbanach is now surrounded by Ardmore Forest) and were in the older settlement of upper **Tobermory** in the late 18th century. Several of these moved to Tiree in the 1830s. Donald MacEachern, baptised at **Erray** in 1811, became a joiner in Tiree, married Mary Cameron there in 1839, and had five sons and one daughter. Many cousins from north east Mull followed Donald to Tiree. From the 1770s the name is widespread in the south west of Mull, in **Knockvologan, Iona, Ardalanish, Kilpatrick** in Ross, **Beach,** and **Scoor**, where a Neil MacEachern was living in 1779, aged 100. MacEachern Christian names were Hugh, Donald, Neil, John, Duncan, Allan and Angus for boys, with an occasional Farquhar and Roderick, while girls were Marys, Floras and Catherines. A Neil MacEachern in **Ardachy**, who married Elizabeth MacLaine in 1813, had nine or ten children, became a widower before 1851, emigrated to Bruce Township, Ontario soon afterwards, and, I am sorry to say, changed his name to MacKechnie!

In 1752 the trustees of John Maclaine of Lochbuie granted tacks to Malcolm, Lachlan and Dougal MacPhaden and their heirs and successors in Kinlochspelve. In 1764 a marriage contract between a Duncan MacPhaden, tenant in **Garmony**, son of Gilbert MacPhaden, and Julian MacLean, niece of Lady Lochbuie, shows that the MacFadyens were going up in the world. In the 1779 ducal census Finlay MacPhaden had two sons, Archie,15 and Neil,10, in **Assapol**, while in nearby **Scoor** John MacPhaden was a grasskeeper with sons Donald,10, Lachlan,8, Neil,6, and Archie,2. In **Kellan** Mill in 1779, Donald MacPhaden was the miller with sons John, 4, and Phaden,1. Such combinations of Christian name and surname are frequent in Mull families, being at first a kind of echo of the old patronymic system of naming, and then, from the habit of naming children after grandparents, becoming, in the case of Phaden, a Christian name in its own right. Archibald MacPhaden, who was probably also the son of Donald the miller, but born about 1784, married Flora MacInnes in the early 1800s, and was still the miller of Kellan in the 1861 census, aged 77. In **Tobermory** in 1851, Angus MacFadyen (for the spelling changed about this time) was a lobster fisher, 47, originally from Kilfinichen parish, with his wife Mary MacKinnon and their six sons, Peter, 20, Archibald,16, Donald,15, Hector,12, John, 8 and Neil, 6. The headland of **Burg** sheltered many MacFadyens in the 19th century, and they spread over the hill into the area of **Gribun**. There was a strong cluster in **Balevulin**. The graveyard at Killiemore House, on the north shore of Loch Scridain provides information about these families. Anyone with an Ebenezer MacFadyen in their family should count themselves fortunate in having such a traceable ancestor, for he must have been the only Ebenezer in Mull, and was son of the **Killiemore** schoolmaster, David MacFadyen. One of the most distinguished MacFadyens was the "well-known Mull bard", nowadays alas not so well-known, John MacFadyen, who was baptised at Balevulin in 1850, son of Donald MacFadyen and Mary MacLachlan. He lived mainly in Glasgow, and his popular writings were collected in *An t-Eileanach*, published in 1890. Concerts or ceilidhs are even now brought to a close with John's song, *Soraidh Leibh is Oidhche Mhath Leibh,* of the "blessings upon you and goodnight" variety.

Clann Pharlain is generally regarded as hailing from Loch Lomond, but whether Mull MacFarlanes came originally from there is hard to determine. In the late 18th century they were in **Ardchiavaig, Ardfenaig, Ardtun, Arle, Ardnacross** and **Iona**, but in fairly modest numbers. There were only about five MacFarlanes in Torosay in the census of 1841, and another five in the quoad sacra parish of Salen. **Tobermory**, that refuge for cottars and crofters who had been evicted from the farming areas of Mull, Morvern and Ardnamurchan, had only one family of this name in 1841 - Duncan, with his wife Flora and six children. **Frachadil**, near Calgary, had Robert, over sixty in 1841. **Ballygown** had Donald with two children, Catherine and Mary. It is not until we look at the people of Ulva in 1841 that we find several families such as John and Sarah with four sons, Hugh, Alexander, John and an unnamed infant, and Donald with his wife Catherine and grown-up children Alexander, Donald and Flora. Both of these families lived in a place which is now only named on the map as a bleak hill - **Eolasary.** Still in Ulva, at **Cragaig**, Andrew MacFarlane was a sixty-year-old crofter and kelper, with his wife Sarah and adult children Donald, Lachlan, Helen and Sarah. In another cottage in Cragaig, Dugald and Effy MacFarlane had two baby sons, Lachlan and Donald. This last family (and no doubt the other three also) was evicted by F.W. Clark of Ulva in 1851, when there were seven children. They went to Tobermory where they were described as "very destitute" when the Highland and Island Emigration Society was making its choice of emigrants in 1852. Fortunately they were accepted, and it is to be hoped that they improved their lot in Australia. It is not often that we can tour Mull looking for a name and find fewer than fifty - but we have not come to the Ross of Mull and Iona in the 1841 census, and it is there that a hundred other MacFarlanes are lurking. Sixteen families lived in **Bunessan, Uisken, Ardfenaig, Ardtun, Assapol, Iona, Kintra** and **Creich.** It is not possible to list a hundred MacFarlanes, but certain outstanding Christian names, such as Parlan, Malcolm, Hugh, Angus, George and Walter for males, and Grace, Elizabeth, Eve and Anne for females might help some descendants to determine their place of origin. Although most Mull people were farmers or crofters, MacFarlanes had a tendency to be boatbuilders, like Hugh in Ardtun, born about 1790, and John in Kintra, born about 1799 and married first to Effy Black, then to Mary MacEachern. Bruce Township in Ontario was the final resting place of many, including James (1838-1905), and Susan (1847-1867), who married James MacCallum before her early death. Ronald in Iona was one of a family who went on the *Marmion* to Australia in 1852, his mother, Mary being described approvingly as a "fine healthy woman". They were almost certainly related to John and Sally MacFarlane from **Leob** in Ardtun, who left Tobermory for Liverpool to sail on the same ship with four sons, Hugh, 19, Alexander, 17, John, 14 and Malcolm, 12, and two daughters Mary, 9, and Flora, 4. Neil MacFarlane, weaver in Iona went to Glenelg, Ontario in the 1840s with his wife Margaret MacEachern, and Mary, Catherine, Alexander, John and Eve. John MacFarlane in Creich was ninety-eight in the census of 1861, but since he had put on sixteen years since the 1851 census, we must treat him with caution. He and his Colonsay wife, Elizabeth MacKenzie had lived in Aird of **Penmore**, in the parish of Kilninian and Kilmore, in their younger days, A granddaughter with the original name of Hillary might alert some descendant to a not irretrievable piece of family history.

With Macdonald, MacDougall, MacFadyen, MacKinnon and Maclean, MacGillivray or MacGilvray is one of the oldest of Mull names. Its provenance which has remained virtually unchanged for six centuries, is the area around Loch Scridain, and the headland of Burg in particular. In letters of caption of 1675, when the earl of Argyll was requesting hundreds of Mull tenants to appear in court, Donald Garve McIlvray and Archibald McIlvray were in **Saorphin**, while Martin Neelchallin McIlvray was in **Ardchiavaig**. Many other MacGilvrays grace the threatening documents of the earls in the late 17th century, with patronymics displaying the full range of family Christian names. When the Campbells of Argyll finally got their way and became possessors of the west of Mull, their estate census of 1779 indicates that the MacGilvrays were not evicted, but remained in exactly the same farms - **Ardtun, Saorphin, Suidhe, Bunessan, Assapol, Knocknafenaig, Shiaba, Iona, Beach, Dererach and Burg,** with the distinctive clan forename of Martin still surviving. In the first twenty years of the 19th century, Neil McGilvra was a tenant in **Killiemor** in the parish of Kilfinichen. He was married to Christina MacEachern, but the baptisms of their children are rather erratic in the parish register, due to the fact that the far side of Loch Scridain was difficult of access for a baptising minister who had to go on horseback to the homes of his flock. Missionaries were always being assigned to this part of the parish, but did not last long, so all MacGilvray ancestor hunters should be warned that at best only a quarter of births are recorded in MacGilvray country. But Neil's son Charles was written down in 1815, even if that was some time after the actual birth. Charles was to become a physician and a distinguished Gaelic scholar who translated *The Pilgrim's Progress* (published in 1869). MacGilvrays, considering they are such an old family, are very little written about. Apart from a number of local people commemorated in the graveyard at Kilfinichen, there are no extant memorials. One family did have the territorial title of "Pennyghael". Alexander of Pennyghael recorded a sasine in 1725, of the lands of Pennyghael, Finachag and Carsaig, and Hugh of Pennyghael, Younger, had this confirmed in 1771. Hugh married Catherine, daughter of John MacLaine of Lochbuie, so that the MacGilvrays of Pennyghael belonged to Mull's gentry. In the 1841 census of the Burg area, ten MacGilvray heads of households had a total of thirty-eight children between them. In the same census there were seventeen MacGilvrays in Shiaba where most of the inhabitants were removed in 1847. Those who survived an epidemic of cholera on their arrival in Canada, settled in Fergus, Ontario. By the 1851 census, the name is still concentrated in the Ross of Mull, belonging to the duke of Argyll, and in **Ardmeanach. Kinloch**, which was owned by Donald MacLean of Kinloch, Writer to the Signet, was a miserable refuge for many who had been pushed out of neighbouring estates, and some of the poorer 'pauperised' MacGilvrays are to be found here. I would say that if you have MacGilvrays in your family, your chances of reconstructing relationships are very slim, for the repetition of Duncans, Neils, Archibalds, Donalds, Catherines, Marions and Marys is even more vexing than in other families. If you are lucky enough to have a Martin it may be plain sailing.

A most difficult name, complicated by the fact that its official proscription from 1603 until 1661, and again from 1693 until 1784, forced its bearers to assume aliases which are sometimes logical and sometimes perverse. Of the first type we have the family who played an important part in the commerce of the island in the 18th and early 19th centuries, the Gregorsons of Ardtornish, in Morvern. Angus Gregorson was tacksman there in 1779 with a family of nine males and seven females, none of whom is named. Meanwhile, in **Auchnacraig**, Torosay, Mull, which included in its bounds **Grass Point**, where the ferry to the mainland operated, John MacGregor was the ferryman, aged 20. The name was the same, but enumerated by different people, it appears variously as Grigorson, Gregorson, MacGregor and McGrigor. The duke of Argyll had the monopoly of ferries on his estates, and had granted the tack of Auchnacraig, with its ferry and its inn, to a succession of Gregorsons of the Ardtornish family. In the 1841 census there were no Gregorsons there, but in 1851 the name had returned in the shape of Dugald McGregor, 58, ferryman, with his wife Catherine, and six daughters, the two youngest being twins. The other Gregorson families on the island in 1841 could be counted on one hand - Peter in **Ardachy**, with his wife Catherine McDonald and Janet, 4 and William, 2. In 1841, three ladies of independent means in **Rossal,** Jessie, Mary and Ann Gregorson are clearly of the Ardtornish family. Then in **Kilpatrick** (Kilfinichen parish), we have James, 50, with wife Marion Shaw, 40 and their children, Mary Ann, 15, Alexander 13, Ann, 10, John, 8, Marion, 6, and Mary, 4, but a little investigation of this family shows that they were originally in **Ardchoirk.** Ardchoirk was one of those townships teeming with people (eighty-three in the duke's census of 1779) which one knows, with hindsight, are ear-marked for population problems in a later generation, and therefore are eventual targets for evictions. In 1779, the tacksman who supplied names for the census had a Donald McYeil, tenant in Ardchoirk, with three sons, Dugald, John and Malcolm. The name has been interpreted as 'McGill', but my own theory is that it is the same as 'McGhiel' which occurs many times in the baptism records of Torosay parish, and in Ardchoirk in particular, in the early 19th century. If one follows the families called McGhiel with enough perseverance, one sees them adopting the name of MacGregor, or perhaps returning to it, if we keep the proscription in mind. A perfect example of this is the family of Malcolm McGhiel and his wife Peggy MacLachlan in Ardchoirk. Ten children were baptised to them in the period 1796-1818. The first eight were McGhiels, but Peggy and Lachlan, baptised in 1815 and 1818 respectively, were entered as MacGregors. This kind of change might lead us to suppose that MacGregor was a later phase for the McGhiels, but for the fact that the old parish register has Alexander MacGregor, married to Anne Fletcher in 1816, changing back to McGhiel! MacGregor descendants looking up computer indexes, should therefore try McGhiel when they are no longer able to locate MacGregors. In 1851 at Ardchoirk a Dugald MacGregor aged 39 is a crofter. He and his wife Mary, also born a MacGregor, have seven sons ranging in age from thirteen down to one, Alexander, Donald, Malcolm, Archibald, Peter, Dugald and Lachlan. Also in 1851, Robert MacGregor in **Balevulin** (near Kilfinichen) was the miller. He was 56, born in Torosay, and had a daughter Ellen, 25, a mantua maker. Ellen is a mystery, because her baptism in 1825 shows her to be Nelly, daughter of James, and Marion Shaw, mentioned above. Perhaps she was unofficially adopted. Such problems are only too common when you try to link people up.

In the duke of Argyll's estate census of 1779, there are four distinct families of McOlphadricks in north west Mull, on the farms of Frachadil, and Pennymore and Aird. The single family in **Frachadil** consisted of Archibald, born about 1734, his wife, and their son Peter aged 13. Aird and Pennymore, that is the farm now called **Penmore,** but stretching northwards to include the Aird, or promontory, had Peter McOlphadrick, a workman of 55, his son Malcolm,18, his wife and three daughters. This Peter, also called Patrick in the registers, used the alias of Campbell, a useful fact to remember when the McIlphadrigs appear to vanish in the 19th century. His wife's name was Mary MacDougall. Another family in Penmore was Lachlan, 43, with son Donald, 21, a wife and two daughters. The third family in Penmore consisted of Donald, 50, with three sons, John,14, Neil,12, and Hugh, 8, and two daughters, who are, like all females in the census of this region, unnamed. This seems to be the same as Donald, married to Katherine Rankin in **Sunipol** in 1769. A cottar with no family in Penmore was another Archibald, 31, who was so recently married to Marion McLucas or MacDougall, that he had not yet had their son Duncan or daughter Anne. If these are the core families of McIlphadrigs, they do not go on to have the large families of five or six, which was the average at the time. This may be because they took up their alias of Campbell, and we cannot find them, but on the other hand, half a century later there were still McIlphadrigs in the 1841 census who inhabited the home ground - **Kilmore**, Penmore and **Tostary,** so that all were not hiding behind the adopted name. By 1851, only three families survived with the old name. These were Hector 'McIlfadrick', 49, in **Tobermory**, who claimed to be born in Torosay (but no record shows such a baptism) with a son and three daughters. Since McIlphadrigs belonged to a fixed part of Mull, stretching from Tostary northwards to Penmore, it follows that when villages were set up, their mecca was **Dervaig**, where several baptisms are recorded in the OPRs, but where no one of the family appears in the censuses of 1841 and later. A John McIlphadrig in **Inivea**, a hillside township overlooking Calgary bay and

belonging to Frachadil, might have been related to the men in the 1779 census. He married Janet Campbell in 1792, had seven children, but had moved to **Reudle** by 1799. Their only son, Donald, baptised in 1796 may be the forty-year-old farmer in Tostary in 1841, for in that census, ages were rounded down to the nearest multiple of five. No unusual Christian names provide easy identifiers for the McIlphadrigs. Like the Campbells, they had few inspirations beyond John and Mary. The large number of Patersons who emerged in Mull in the 19th century were almost certainly McIlphadrigs.

MACINNES

Sometimes rendered MacInnish, it can be strangely unrecognisable with only a letter changed, so that James Boswell's meeting with a man called "MacGinnis" on Iona is quite disconcerting. **Iona** indeed holds the largest concentration of MacInneses. In 1779 there were forty five of them, forming about one fifth of the population. Naturally, the neighbouring Ross of Mull had MacInneses, at **Knockvologan, Creich, Ardfenaig**, and **Bunessan**. **Kinloch**, at the head of Loch Scridain, and **Kilfinichen** on the northern shores of the same loch had a few, but although the name faded away as you went eastwards, there were still enough in Kilninian and Torosay parishes to be the exception to the rule. Robert McInnes in

Salen died in 1857, a Chelsea pensioner aged 97, having been married to an Achadashenaig girl, Mary Carmichael in 1792. As the seventh most common name on Mull and Iona, it would be difficult to list all the mainstream MacInneses. The batch recorded as having gone to Eldon Township, Ontario about 1840 from the Ross of Mull, headed by Archibald, were from **Fidden.** Archibald's wife, Ketty MacQuarrie, was one of an extended family of MacQuarries in Tirghoil in the first quarter of the 19th century. The Knockvologan MacInneses, Sandy, Dugald, Allan and John, who were young  boys in 1779, were probably the ancestors of the group of MacInneses who stayed around **Fionnphort** and **Kintra**, and were to be innkeepers and the ferrymen for travellers to Iona in the 1840s. Iona, which had sixteen families of MacInneses in the 1841 census, had lost 50% of them by the 1851 census, and most of the lost ones are accounted for in E. Mairi MacArthur's authoritative book, *Iona, the living memory of a crofting community, 1750-1914.* One of these, the infant teacher, beadle and precentor Neil MacInnes, son of Malcolm, and his wife Mary Black, had married in 1836. Their infant son John died in 1839, in 1845 their four-year-old daughter Mary fell over a precipice, and in 1848 another daughter died. It is small wonder that they moved to Canada in 1849 to start a new life. Another Iona schoolmaster, Dugald MacInnes, his wife Mary Campbell from Tiree, who had married in 1838, and their two children went to Canada in 1853. Donald MacInnes, schoolmaster in **Gribun**, and his wife Helen MacLachlan, married in 1816, had a son Archibald who became the Free Church schoolmaster at **Aridhglas** in the Ross of Mull. In the 1861 census, Donald the father is a widower of 83, cared for by four unmarried mature children including Archibald. With the nearby MacCormick school-masters' families at Catchean, all guarding their mature offspring also, this collection of teachers' sons and daughters must have given the local club of Thirty Somethings a remarkable flavour. The abundance of Iona and Ross of Mull MacInneses cannot begin to be adequately covered. MacInneses from Kilninian and Kilmore parish are to be found in broad areas of north west Mull in 1779, with concentrations in **Corkamull, Killiemor, Kellan, Sorne** and **Frachadil**. By 1851 there are still several MacInnes families at Sorne, but in the following decade Mr James Forsyth, proprietor of Glengorm Castle, and as ruthless an evictor as F.W. Clark of Ulva, swept the estate clean of people. In the 1850s it was best to be in an island fastness like **Little Colonsay**, where Archibald MacInnes, 82, lived with his lobster fisher son Duncan, and his family, or Iona, where, as I have said, MacInneses disappeared, but without all the unpleasantness of the Forsythian methods.

MACINTYRE

When Alexander MacIntyre, Ardalanish, gave evidence to Lord Napier in the course of the inquiry into the condition of the crofters and cottars of the highlands and islands, in August 1883, he claimed that his ancestors had held land under the family of Argyll for three hundred years. This was not entirely accurate, for the Campbells of Argyll had been overlords for less than two hundred years. But there were certainly MacIntyres at Loch Scridain in a document of 1675, and before 1775 they possessed**Ardalanish**. Malcolm, 40, was a tenant of Ardalanish in 1779 with three sons, Neil, John and Peter, and three daughters, who are unnamed. At the same time, Nicol MacIntyre, 58 was a tenant there, with sons Donald and Duncan and three daughters. Duncan MacIntyre, son of Nicol, became a Baptist about 1822 after at least six of his own children had been baptised in the conventional manner, began composing hymns in 1850, and published a volume in Gaelic in 1857. In the 1850s, Duncan and his wife Mary Maclean, both aged about 80, moved to **Knockvologan** with their two unmarried middle-aged sons, Nicol and Neil. Duncan, Mary, and Neil all died in 1863, leaving Nicol to enter the sear and yellow leaf alone. MacIntyres tended to live to a ripe old age, like the other Duncan in **Ardchrishnish** who died in 1862 aged 93. They are buried in Kilpatrick (Ross of Mull) burial ground. Yet another Duncan MacIntyre was a heritor from 1844, when he bought the estate of Burg. In spite of appearances, not all Mull MacIntyres came from the Ross of Mull. The shepherd Joseph MacIntyre, who lived at **Tavool** in 1851 and near **Fidden** in 1861, and was married to Jessie McColl, with six children, claimed that he was born at Pennygown in 1805. A shepherd called Nicol MacIntyre who was born in 1810 in Torosay parish, married Janet MacDougall about 1838 and had at least five children. Latterly they were in the overcrowded township of **Ardchoirk**, near Gorten, before paying £27 to the Highland and Island Emigration Society and sailing on the *Panama* for Tasmania in 1853. Norman MacIntyre, a farmer at **Lephein**, near Ardmore bay, north of Tobermory, was prosperous enough to pay his family's passage on the *New Zealander* to Victoria in 1853, but not daring enough to declare his real age to the emigration society, for he was 56 according to the census, and 46 in the society's books. His children were Alexander, Janet, Flora, Peter and James. The one-year-old Peter MacIntyre son of that early Malcolm in Ardalanish of whom we spoke, had a complex, but well-documented life in Ardalanish, **Lee** and **Knocknafenaig**. His mother turned out to be Flora Campbell. Peter married Euphemia MacKinnon in 1807, and after the births of two daughters, Euphemia died. Peter married Flora Bell in 1812. He and Flora had six children by 1823, but I suspect that like their relation, Duncan, they became Baptists and stopped believing in infant baptism, for Euphemia, born about 1825 is not in the baptism records. Peter, like many of his name, lived to the respectable age of 89 and died at Knocknafenaig in 1867. Intriguing MacIntyre names, as you will have observed, are Nicol, Peter, Duncan and Walter for boys and Rachel, Dorothy, Flora and Clementina for girls. The Campbells would have done well to copy a little of this style, but it was only when a family had used up all the grandparents' names that they could afford to be fanciful.

I hesitate to leave this name out of a book on Mull surnames, as it seems to embody a whole pattern of development common to other Mull names. It has an archaic sound, and yet it is very difficult to find examples of the name in rentals and lists before 1750. At **Aros**, Gilbert McKeallich married Ann Black in 1768. Only three of their children appear in the parish register - Donald baptised in 1773, Duncan in 1775 and Ann in 1785, but a John appears in the duke of Argyll's census, who must have been born in 1769. At **Killiechronan**, John McKealach in the Duke's census in 1779 aged 40 does not appear in the baptism register at all, but his sons were John, 15, Duncan, 10 and Hugh, 3. However, nearly all the other MacKellaichs who do get married or baptised in the parish of Kilninian are in **Sorne**. Again we have a Duncan, marrying Beatrix MacFarlane in 1794, and because Duncan was a fencible man, and is absent when his first child, Mary, was baptised in 1795, a sponsor has to take the vows. Four more children, Donald, Catherine, Neil and Robert were baptised by 1815, and we cannot tell whether Duncan lost his life in the French wars, or emigrated after his return, but he and his Beatrix have gone. In 1851 the census was taken on the 30 March, and two fine McKellaich families were in Sorne - Angus and Kate with four young children, and John and Janet with five. Three hundred souls were evicted from Sorne on Whitsunday of that year, but both of our families were spared, for they reappear in 1861. Following through to 1871, Kate has been widowed, she has Hugh, 26 and Margaret, 16 with her, but John and Janet have vanished. In **Tobermory** in 1851, a joiner, John McKellaich has a wife called Sally or Sarah, and six children, including David and Henry, which should allow any descendants to identify them. And now for the bad news. It is said, although I cannot confirm it from any of my searches for these families, that McKellaichs from Mull simply decided (cf. MacEachern and MacGregor) to call themselves Macdonald. One would have thought that with so many Johns among them, they might have opted for McIan 'son of John', but nothing in the adoption of names is logical. If you have Macdonalds in your tree, and you are entirely at a stalemate, you could try a brief look at McKellaichs, remembering to spell it every way you can imagine. I hope it helps.

Not a strong contestant for inclusion as a Mull name, as it was a comparatively late incomer. John MacKenzie, 64, was the innkeeper at **Aros** in 1779 with a son Duncan, 36. Readers of Johnson and Boswell may be interested in my speculation that this Duncan was the husband of Miss Maclean, who charmed Dr Johnson with her accomplishments and who was described by Boswell as "a little plump elderly young lady". Miss Maclean's parents would not approve of such an unequal marriage, but the lady had a mind of her own, and did marry a man called Duncan MacKenzie in 1786, only months after her father's death. As the widowed Mrs MacKenzie, she was visited by travellers to Mull, but there were no children from the marriage, so that genealogically speaking, this information is not helpful. The only other family of Mackenzies in the 1779 census lived at **Oskamull,** and if I may speculate still further (a practice I would strongly discourage in my readers), the chances are that Angus MacKenzie, 34, who married Janet MacColl in 1767, was the brother of Duncan. Angus did have a large family of ten children, of whom eight were sons, John, Hugh, Duncan, Archibald, Hugh, John, Duncan and Donald. When a Christian name is repeated in a family, it does suggest that the first of the name died, but this cannot always be assumed. Angus's second Duncan was baptised at **Erray** in 1791. Again, you have to be a Johnson and Boswell addict to obtain a frisson from this, for if Mrs MacKenzie and her husband stayed at Erray (where Johnson and Boswell had met her) after Dr Hector Maclean's death, they may have taken in their MacKenzie relations. What a wonderful aunt Mrs Mackenzie would have been to this band of children! But, coming back to earth with a bump, I have to add that there were other MacKenzies in Mishnish in the last quarter of the 18th century who do not appear in the 1779 census because the duke of Argyll did not own Mishnish. These families lived in **Rairaig, Ardmore, Penalbanach** and **Sorne,** and in 1783 there is a record of a marriage in 'Tobermorrie' of Kenneth MacKenzie and Marion Stewart, who had entered into an irregular and clandestine marriage in 1781, being conducted in a more regular and solemn manner. The estate of **Torloisk** was also not in the 1779 census, and there William MacKenzie and Margaret Rankin from Kilbrenan (likely to be from the family of pipers there), had two natural children before marrying in a regular way in 1769. Three groups of MacKenzies in **Tobermory** in the 1851 census were born in Ardnamurchan, reminding us that Ardnamurchan was cleared in one fell swoop by Sir James Riddell in 1828, and that these were refugees from the evictions. Ewen MacKenzie, the merchant and grocer from Ardnamurchan who traded in Portmore, Tobermory, was born in about 1803, and had eight children born in Mull between 1830 and 1850. By 1851 the native breed of MacKenzies, if we can call the 18th century ones 'natives', seems to have vanished from the island, leaving only MacKenzie Street in Tobermory as a very transitory memento. One hundred and thirty-three people shared this address in 1851.

McGilp and McKillop are the same name. If this difference in spelling exists at the same time, for instance in the 1779 census, it is only because two different tacksmen were acting as enumerators for the chamberlain of Mull, who organised the exercise. The one in Iona spelt the name McGilp, and the one in Auchnacroish, Torosay, spelt it McKillop. Both stabilised as McKillop eventually. Apart from the usual excess of Johns, the most common Christian name for McKillops was Colin. A Colin was the innkeeper at **Craignure**, in that very same inn you can see today. A Colin in **Achnacroish** in 1845, married to Anne Campbell, had twin sons Donald and Colin.

A Colin in Iona in the census of 1851 lived at Lagandorain. He was 76 years old. His wife Margaret MacEachern was 75. They had been married in 1806, Margaret being one of the **Ardachy** MacEacherns. Their children were all girls, and had pretty names - Rachel, Catherine, Isabel, Hester, Margaret and Flora. MacKillops in Torosay parish were connected mostly with **Ardchoirk**, and married into typical Ardchoirk families such as Buchanans and MacGregors. John MacKillop in Ardchoirk married Marion or Sarah MacColl before 1795 and had at least five children, including twins. In **Tobermory**, in 1851, Donald MacKillop in Argyll Terrace was born in Lorn, but his wife Mary MacGregor was a Torosay woman, and their children, Archibald, Mary, Alexander, Catherine, Isabella and John were all born in Mull. I think that the message of this entry is that apart from the Iona strain, all roads lead back to Ardchoirk.

Mackinnon is one of our truly original Mull names, although it shares its antiquity and currency with Skye. But this is easily explained by the fact that the Mackinnon chiefs in Mull were also lairds in Skye, and derived their territorial titles from Skye. The six Mull clan heads who attended the meeting in Aros in 1608, which was a preliminary to the enacting of the *Statutes of Iona,* included Mackinnon of Mackinnon, a Skye chief with subsidiary lands in Mishnish in Mull. Mackinnon lairds may have been less interested in Mull than in Skye (and who could blame them?), but if so they were in the same position as the Macleans of Coll, who used their Mull territory of Quinish as a stepping stone to the mainland. In 1711, John McKinvine (Mackinnon) of Strathardell, and his baillie in Mull, Neil McKinvine, shook the Collector of the Assize Tax on Herring until his bones rattled for attempting to hold a court in Mishnish, and when the case was tried at Inveraray, they were found to be in the right. So hemmed in were they by Argyll Campbells that many Campbells forgot that Mishnish was another property. Yet Mishnish was a sad reduction of their old power in Mull, and all over the island Mackinnons were being pushed into marginal lands as the Campbells gained power. Numerically, they were strong, but few were, by the 18th century, of the tenant class. James Boswell commented that the "strange confused house" he and Dr Johnson slept in at Erray, near Tobermory, was built by Mackinnon "about sixty years ago" - so by the very same 'McKinvine' who had been so incensed by Campbells holding court on his land! This house, Old Erray, still stands today, the remains of the Mackinnon empire. The name of Mackinnon was so widespread in Mull in our period, that I cannot begin to cite examples of it, as there was no place, with the exception perhaps of the area around Lochbuie and Duart, where Mackinnons were not legion. They were densest on the poorest soils, such as **Ardmeanach**, and they never seemed to have sprung from anywhere but Mull, marrying within their own locality. The most illustrious Mackinnon, whose parents came from the Loch Scridain/Brolass area, although he was born in Colonsay, was Professor Donald Mackinnon, (1839-1914), first Professor of Celtic at Edinburgh University from 1882. His great-aunt, Catherine Mackinnon, was a nurse or governess to the children of one of the Czars. All the popular Mull Christian names are in the Mackinnon genealogies - although Angus is rarer than most, so if your ancestor is an Angus you might have a chance of succeeding with a family tree. An Angus, (1800-1874) married to Mary Black in **Ardtun**, went to Canada, where he died in 1874. For some reason there are many girls called Rebecca. After the Mackinnons lost Mishnish, the clan pined for a leader, and Walter Scott describes how he met a "Mackinnon of Mackinnon", a young gentleman born and bred in England but nevertheless a Highland chief at Aros, "anxious to buy back some of the family property which was sold long since". This young gentleman turned later into William Alexander Mackinnon, MP for Lymington, and did become the nominal chief of the clan, although he did not buy back Mishnish in Mull or become a father to his clansmen in the old sense, in spite of a petition signed by one hundred and fifty-three Mackinnons in Skye in 1848, pleading for his 'return'.

It is tempting to suppose that Maclachlans came into Mull quite late from mainland Argyll, sailing across by the shortest route, and settling in the environs of Duart Castle where they are, to put it mildly, legion. But a list of tenants in a rental of 1662 has Mr Neil McLachlan in Duart paying a rent of one hundred marks. A Donald McLauchlan in Icolumkill (Iona) was denounced a rebel by the earl of Argyll in 1675. It looks as if the name was well settled in Mull before the beginning of the 18th century. The chief Christian names for boys were Lachlan, Dugald, Archibald and the ubiquitous John, which makes it difficult to effect any continuity. The two late 18th century strongholds of the MacLachlans were **Killean** and **Auchnacraig**, and although we find a greater spread of MacLachlans across Mull by the middle of the 19th century, many are descended from these Torosay parish families. One who was not was Dugald McLachlan Esquire, of Killiemor, heritor, owner of the beautiful Kilfinichen mansion of **Killiemor** on the north side of Loch Scridain. He was the son of Eun McLachlan of Laudle in Morvern, and he married, judiciously, Isabella Stewart of Achadashenaig. Their children numbered ten, and while one could write a book about this family alone, I shall content myself with telling you that their third daughter, Catherine Maxwell McLachlan, married Francis William Clark, Younger of Ulva, a young lawyer who showed a certain amount of retrospective embarrassment about his father's multiple evictions. A most impressive number of McLachlans in Mull were blacksmiths, beginning with Robert in **Ardachy** in 1779 aged 34. Another Robert in Ardachy was a smith when he married Mary MacDonald in 1823. They emigrated to Canada in about 1831. Donald McLachlan (1805-1889) was a blacksmith in Ardachy, then in **Creich** who, with his wife Annabella McDonald, had ten children. The family had connections through marriage with the Grahams and the MacCormicks. Donald retired to **Ballygown** in Kilninian, and died there in 1889, but according to Donald Beaton's evidence to Lord Napier in 1883 his place was taken from him. Yet another blacksmith was Alexander who although born in Morvern about 1805, was in **Ulva** from 1840 into the 1860s. Hugh McLachlan was the smith in **Bunessan** in the 1830s and married Ann Beaton there in 1837. A tailor in the ducal census of 1779 of Aros, was Archibald McLachlan, 38, who, we know from the parish register, married Giles Campbell in 1778. Their sons Duncan, Alexander and John were born in 1784, 1785 and 1787, but are not identifiable afterwards. Dugald McLachlan, tacksman in Auchnacraig was a shadowy figure who had a large family bearing so many of the McLachlan names that it is difficult to connect them, although connected they must be, with the scores of McLachlans in the area. A man who raised a remarkable family was Dugald McLachlan, (1814-1865), prison keeper in **Tobermory,** married to Ann Mcphail, with nine children, Alexander (who became a physician), John, Andrew (who went to Massachusetts), Dugald, Nancy, Margaret, Donald, Archibald and Susan. The Clan MacLachlan Society is very active in reconstructing its families and its present chairman is a mine of information. **Penalbanach**, north west of Tobermory, held a clutch of McLachlans in the 1780s and 1790s - Peter or Patrick, married to Mary McInnes, John married to Catherine MacLucas, and Duncan married to Catherine MacMillan or McIlvoil, who married in 1780 and had Mary, Duncan, Janet, Donald, Jean, Mary and Murdoch. Returning to the heartland, we can point out the marriage of John (son of Hugh, the innkeeper at Auchnacraig) with Catherine Buchanan in 1810. This produced eight children in Killean, three of whom, Alexander, Hugh and Neil, emigrated to Ontario.

MACLAINE

It is nearly impossible to treat Mull's Top Name like any other entry, for it would take a very large book to do it justice. Several books have been written on the Macleans, chief among them being A. Maclean Sinclair's *The Clan Gillean*, published in Charlottetown, Prince Edward Island in 1899. This author was concerned mainly with the aristocracy, the smaller lairds, and those Macleans with territorial titles. Nicholas Maclean Bristol has embarked on a history of the clan with a first volume, published in 1995, entitled *Warriors and Priests*, which takes us to 1570. Because I am speaking of Mull alone, I have divided the clan into Maclaines and Macleans in spite of a comment in the preface that spelling does not matter, that Macs can change overnight to Mcs, and that we are probably speaking of the same family regardless. But in the case of the difference between Maclaine and Maclean, spelling is significant, for the former indicates a connection with the Lochbuie family, while the latter would refer to others - all stemming perhaps from equally noble beginnings. Before 1750 letters from members of the Lochbuie family are signed in many different ways, but with a tendency towards Maclaine. It is said that after the accession of John Maclaine of Lochbuie in 1751, he deliberately adhered to the spelling "Maclaine", and this is borne out by his signature in a quite archaic hand on many extant documents. Members of the Lochbuie family, if they were still quite far out, signed themselves "Maclean" in the mid-18th century, but as if in response to the road sign "Get in lane", they began to use the Lochbuie spelling too, so that when Murdoch 19th of Lochbuie came

into the estate rather unexpectedly through the murder of his cousin Archie in 1784, he was already making the distinction. Tenants of the Lochbuie estates in the reign of the irascible John 17th of Lochbuie included his illegitimate son Gillean Maclaine (c.1724-1788) who married Maria MacQuarrie of Ulva in 1771, and had twelve children, ten of whom survived. Their house at Scallastle might be said to have competed with Moy House as a centre of Lochbuie operations. It was more accessible, was halfway between Grass Point and Aros, and on the tourist route to Staffa. Gillean, although living part of the year in Edinburgh as a lawyer, ran estate affairs and dealt with tenants in a more civilised manner than his father, who was known to attack commoners with a whip. With the advent of Murdoch 19th in 1785, the building of a new Moy House in 1790, the continued exile of the landless Duart Macleans and the continuing dynasty of the Scallastle family after Gillean's death in 1788, the Maclaines of Lochbuie were the most prestigious family in Mull. While the Macleans of Torloisk, the Macleans of Coll at Quinish, the Macleans of Brolass (who inherited the title of Chief and the baronetcy) and many other Macleans were important, the Maclaines had clout. When the Lochbuie tacksmen and factors wrote down their lists of tenants they wrote their own Macleans as Maclaines. The session clerks and ministers may have been less punctilious in making the distinction, for their parishes were to them seamless robes, even if the duke of Argyll had a long arm shooting into Lochbuie property at Achnacroish and Kilpatrick. Thus all the Macleans on Lochbuie lands between about 1750 and 1850 were written down as Maclaine by people in the know. But when spelling finally stabilised in the later 19th century, many Macleans possibly gave up explaining the difference, and took the easy option. The present representative of the Maclaines of Lochbuie lives in South Africa, and uses the Maclaine spelling, of course. I hope that there are many more descendants overseas who do the same.

Sometimes Maclean numbers, even after the 17th century purges, seem too large to have been accomplished by natural increase. Presenting Maclaine and Maclean separately, but giving no individual treatment to any other spellings, may lighten the load, but still cannot do justice to either of the versions of the name. The following example of a perceived difference between Maclaines and Macleans is simply a change from the customary story of the two brothers, Lachlan and Hector, which is usually told. In 1804, Lachlan Macquarie, later of New South Wales, tried to extricate himself from a scrape with the Army office. He and his uncle, Murdoch Maclaine of Lochbuie

had allowed Murdoch's son John to be put forward for a commission at the age of nine. When they were in danger of being exposed, they considered substituting an older John Maclean for John Maclaine. Lachlan wrote to Murdoch that Mr John Maclean might have the commission "providing he is willing to personate him and write his name Maclaine instead of Maclean to which I suppose he will have no objection..." Happily, they did not resort to this scheme, and Mr John Maclean did not pass himself off as a Maclaine, but the story demonstrates the very real difference between the families at that time. In the parishes of Kilninian and most of Kilvickeon, Macleans were Macleans, with the Macleans of Brolass, Torloisk and Coll being the principal landowners. In the Torloisk area, the 1841 census shows a remarkable concentration of Macleans from **Burg** to **Fanmore**, **Ballygown** and **Kilbrennan**. One presumes that they are descendants of followers of the Torloisk family. Although the Marquis of Northampton, who inherited the estate through the maternal line, does not have the name of being a cruel evictor, Mrs Marianne Douglas Maclean Clephane did a little weeding out which went unnoticed in the 1820s and 1830s, and Northampton took advantage of the Highland and Island Emigration Society's endeavours to part with some tenants in the 1850s. Hugh Maclean,49, in Fanmore, with his wife Sally, 44 and John, 17, Catherine, 15, Donald, 13, Archibald, 8 and Allan,4, a "good family", went to Australia in 1854. Archibald in Ballygown, 41, with a wife Jessie an outstanding dairy-woman, and healthy children, was selected for the same voyage to Portland Bay. In the Ross of Mull, Alexander Maclean at **Ardfenaig** was given a financially unaided passage in spite of having "rather too many young children", because of his wife's relationship to McPhails and McDiarmids who were already chosen. However, these 19th century emigrants were small in number compared to the exodus of Macleans to North America in the previous century. As the preface explains, the earlier emigrations were from the better-off families, and groups such as the Macleans of **Scoor, Uisken,** Ardfenaig and **Bunessan** were decimated by these voluntary removals, with those remaining often being subsidised by the departed ones. A second wave of emigrations in the mid-19th century brought the remaining branches to Canada. A thousand stories are there to tell about the Macleans who went to Canada, such as Charles, son of Donald of Kinloch, who, blinded in youth, and barred from the ministry, married Jane Jessie Campbell in Canada in 1837 and had ten children. Charles (1806-1872) must have so many descendants susceptible to the family story of his having been blinded in a chemistry experiment at university, that it is tempting to issue an official denial. Another temptation which I am succumbing to, is to quote in English the Gaelic saying about

Maclean forenames: "Like a dog lapping soup the names of the Macleans, Eachunn, Lachunn, Tearlach" (Hector,Lachlan,Charles).

The Macleods, Clann 'Ic Leoid, may be significant in Skye and Lewis, but they were smaller fry in Mull. Two families in **Ardnacross** and **Arle** in 1779 were headed by a Roderick McLeod, but Roderick in Arle is more interesting to genealogists because he had two sons, Angus and Lachlan and six unnamed daughters. Still in 1779, a John McLeod in **Penmore** had sons Donald, 14, Neil, 6 and Charles, 2. Charles is of great interest because the name is unusual enough, and the age near enough to identify him with a Charles in **Inivea** who married Catherine McNiven in April 1806. It is always exciting to find a family who lived in Inivea, because this hillside township above Calgary bay is one of the few in Mull sufficiently intact to imagine life within it. Charles and Catherine had a splendid family - John baptised in 1807, Colin in 1809, Alexander in 1811, Neil in 1812, Catherine in 1815, Archibald in 1817, Donald in 1819, Christina in 1822 and Hector in 1824. Only between Christina's birth and Hector's had they moved to **Caliach,** just north east of Inivea and still on the Calgary estate. Charles's brother Neil is likely to have been the Neil in Inivea who married Janet MacLucas in 1802, and had a Catherine baptised in 1803, John, 1807, Mary, 1812 and Barbara in 1817. Both Charles and Neil disappear from the records, as people did when they stopped breeding, but also as they did when they were evicted. Calgary was cleared of thirty-two families in the 1830s. Some went to America, and some to Australia according to the Poor Law Enquiry of 1843. I leave these MacLeods with my readers at this point, and go on to the 1841 census when there were nineteen households of the name of McLeod in the whole island. Notable among them were Norman McLeod senior and Norman junior in **Grass Point,** aged 55 and 25 respectively. Norman junior was the innkeeper, but had disappeared by 1851. His father, however, with his wife Sarah MacKinnon, and their adult children Mary, Robert, Lachlan, Jessie and Sarah, was in the 1851 census at nearby **Ardchaoil,** and Norman senior was there as a widower in 1861 with the still unmarried Robert, Janet and Lachlan. Now aged 77, he farmed six hundred acres. Norman and Sarah had been married in 1811 by the famous minister of St Columba's, Glasgow, Norman MacLeod. Perhaps a relationship can be construed? Dr Norman's father, Norman MacLeod was minister of Morvern from 1775 until 1824, and whether he influenced the choice of Norman as a name, or whether it was simply one of these names which was traditional and hereditary, we cannot say. It was certainly well-used in Mull. Norman in **Creich,** near present-day Fionnphort, born in 1831, was the son of Angus McLeod and Margaret McGilvra. His mother died in 1837, one day after giving birth to Norman's sister Margaret. It was this sister Margaret who seems to have ensured the survival of the Creich McLeods, for by 1871 the brothers John and Norman have been lured from the sea by the siren of the quarry at Tormore. They remained unmarried, and were uncles to Margaret's four children, including a six-year-old Elispey MacDonald. Two daughters of the Rev. Neil MacLeod, host to Dr Johnson and Mr Boswell in 1773, were to be found in Mull in the 19th century - Susanna who married Captain Dugald Maclean of **Ardfenaig** in 1804, was five at the time of the famous visit, and her sister Mary, aged 84 in Springbank, **Tobermory** in 1851, was said to be the last person alive to remember the sage. Also living in Ardfenaig in a different style from Susanna, was William McLeod, (c.1799-   ) a crofter, married to Ann McLean. Their son Hector died in Bruce Township, Ontario in 1894.

Before reading about the MacLucases, you should read the MacDougall entry, and also the note in the preface about problems with names. I have mentioned the name in connection with MacDougalls because people who are very intense genealogists and who have failed to get their MacDougalls back before 1830 could not possibly be expected to know that these two names are sometimes interchangeable, although some MacLucases did manage to cling to their rather attractive name without bowing to expediency. In some records you will also find McClugash as a variant spelling of MacLucas. The tacksman who compiled the Kilninian and Kilmore parish part of the duke of Argyll's list of tenants in 1779 chose this form. Most of these families lived in the area between Calgary and Dervaig, with John McClugash, a cowan (dyke-builder) aged 42 as the principal family man in **Aird,** Penmore. John married Ann Maclean and had five sons by 1779 - Dugald, 12, John, 10, Charles, 7, Neil, 4 and Duncan, 1. In the 1841 census of **Penmore** there were still five families of this name who were probably dispersed in Mr McNab's clearance of 1857. In **Auchnacraig**, Torosay parish, where relationships were not explained in 1779, seven McLugases or McLucashes dwelt. In **Torrans**, in Brolass, a John McLucass was a merchant, aged 60 in 1779. By the time of the national census of 1851, MacLucases in **Ardtun** in the Ross of Mull had gone on to the Poor Roll, but by 1861, most had

made a partial recovery from the ills which followed the potato blight. If you are looking for MacDougall forebears you will have a problem pursuing all these variant forms and spellings in computer indexes. To give you an idea of the scope of the 'merger', the number of families, as opposed to individuals, in Mull called MacDougall in 1851 was about fifty, and the number of MacLucases sixteen.

MACMILLAN

Some Mull MacMillans were also known as McIlvoils in 18th century records, as is demonstrated by Catherine McIlvoil who married Duncan McLauchlan in Penalbanach in 1780. This was an anglicised version of the Gaelic name MacGhilleMhaoil. MacMillans, were, at this time, distributed fitfully and sparsely around the island, in **Arle**, **Achronich**, **Treshnish**, Arin, **Iona**, **Tir Fhearagain** and **Ardchoirk**. Archibald and Flora MacMillan who had both been born in Kilninian parish in about 1790, and who lived on the Strathallan estate at **Oskamull**, embarked on the *New Zealander* in August 1853 for Portland Bay with Ann, 29, Christian, 27, John, 23, and Alexander, 18. The comment on their suitability was "Poor cottar, hale man, eligible family". His next door neighbour Allan Lamont and family went on the same ship. Two Donald MacMillans who were known as McIlvoil married Ann Maclean in 1774 and Marion MacPherson in 1788 respectively. Another McIlvoil called Duncan married Effy Stewart in 1792 and lived at **Sorne** with children Murdoch, John, Ann and Hugh and a child whose name the minister forgot on the way home to the register. MacMillans in **Creich**, by the Sound of Iona had the name Finlay in the family, suggesting a connection with the soldier Finlay who lived at Tir Fhearagain but was away in the wars at the 1779 census. Interesting girls names in the clan were Elrig, Rachel and Charlotte. It is a little disturbing to see an alias for Neil MacMillan in **Killiechronan**, who married Margaret McKay in 1768. Their daughter "Jean, baptised in 1773 was entered as Jean, lawful daughter of Niel McIntaylor alias McMillan". McIntaylour was a surname quite common in Kintyre, which eventually became Taylor. The only other Taylor I know of in Mull is Francis William Taylor who was born at Ardchrishnish (south shore of Loch Scridain) and was pastor of the Baptist Church at Bunessan from 1913 to 1919, so perhaps the alias was confined to Neil. On the whole the MacMillans, including my ancestress Mary MacMillan who was born in 1750, married John MacCallum in Ensay in 1773, and went off to live in **Ardtun**, originated in the north west coast of Mull. Hector MacMillan in **Tobermory** who married Jean McArthur in 1802 seemed to disappear from the records after 1817 with seven children.

MACNEILL

A Mull rental of 1662 provides evidence that there were McNeills in the Ross of Mull in the 17th century. Malcolm McNeill in **Ardfenaig** and Neil McNeill in **Tir Fhearagain**, as well as Gilbert and Donald Ban McNeill in **Uisken,** cannot be linked to any subsequent McNeills, but their forenames are prominent in later McNeill families. Because old parish registers in the parish of Kilninian and Kilmore were kept from 1766, we have the false impression of a weighting of the name in that parish. MacNeills were like sea pinks. They grew on the sea coast from **Aird** to **Sunipol** to **Lag** to **Caliach** to **Calgary** to **Treshnish** to **Reudle** to **Tostary** to **Fanmore** to **Ballygown**, then they crossed the mouth of Loch na Keal and appeared again in **Gribun** and **Ardmeanach**. Travellers in search of McNeill ancestors should begin at Dervaig and travel this route, stopping to go in search of **Caliach.** Here in 1799 a John McNeil married a Marion McNeill (McNeills, more than any other clan were terribly keen on marrying each other!) and between 1799 and 1825 they had a most prodigious family, even by Mull standards, of eleven children, Hector, Donald, Archibald, Charles, Louisa, John, Janet, James, Alexander, Colin and Allan. Not content with giving this family to the community at Caliach, John's relation, probably a brother, Malcolm, born about 1750, the miller (of grain) at Caliach married Janet Campbell in 1784, and had Mary, Catherine, Neil, and Marion before the touching entry in the parish register - "3 November 1799, Malcolm McNeil in Caliach and his deceast wife Janet Campbell had Yr daughter Janet baptised". If you lose your wife, and you have five children to bring up, you remarry pretty quickly, and by 1801 Malcolm had married Ann MacDonald, who bore him Catherine, John, Neil, Charles and Marion. If you are confused by this repetition of names, I have to tell you that these are the authentic McNeill names, and their fancier names like Torquil and Grace are rather exceptional. But we are often lucky with reconstructions from a variety of sources with this surname. For instance there is a good record for Angus McNeill in **Kilmore**, who married Marion McPhail in 1772, after conceiving a natural daughter Mary at the end of 1771. The couple went on to have Kate in 1773, John in 1775, another Mary (suggesting the first child died) in 1777, twins Donald and Catherine in 1779 and Grizel in 1781. The ducal census of 1779 then takes up the story, and we find that Angus at 46 was the innkeeper at **Ledaig**, Tobermory. Ages are fairly reliable in the estate census, with John, baptised in 1775 being 4 and Donald 1. Girls are counted, but not named, but as there was a nurse and a wife and two daughters, we can calculate that a Catherine and a Mary survived thus far. Another Angus McNeill was in **Burg**, Ardmeanach when he married Mary McDonald in 1825. This too was a shotgun wedding, and Angus, who was a shoemaker, left Burg for the bright lights of Tobermory in 1839. We find them in the 1841 census in overcrowded Breadalbane Street, where Angus was 45, Mary, 35, Mary 15, Archibald, 10, Catherine, 10, Eliza, 7, Lachlan, 5 and John, 3. In 1843 the Poor Law Enquiry's commissioners visited the house and put the family in the spotlight. Angus had lost three children from fever, and had five children left, who begged for food. It was a story only too common in Tobermory, but one which has no ending so far, as Angus was not around for the 1851 census. In **Frachadil** Charles McNeill married Florence McNeill in 1772. Donald McNeill and Christina McNeill in Caliach were married before 1808. Donald McNeill and Janet McNeill in Fanmore married in 1776 and were heard of no more. Lachlan McNeill in Balevulin married Flora McNeill before 1800. Donald McKinniker "alias McNeill" in **Killiechronan** gives a clue about possible name changes.

MACPHAIL

A remarkable family by Mull standards, for Mull people were rarely thought of as resourceful or entrepreneurial while they were in Mull, although many of them became so as soon as they went overseas. The name was common in the Highlands from Inverness to Islay, but suddenly appeared in Mull without having appeared in any documents there before 1740. The first mention I have been able to find is a baptism in the Kilninian Old Parish Register on 22 September 1766 to John Macphail and Mary Campbell at **Tenga** of a daughter named Ann, while in the same year John Macphail and Katherine Macpherson in **Achronich** had a son Alexander. Angus Macphail and Janet Campbell were married in 1767, but never heard of again. The Campbells of Argyll, who were so fond of issuing lists of outlaws and rebels in the 17th century, do not include Macphails, but the duke of Argyll's 1779 census of his Mull estates has Colin Macphail, 35, and Malcolm Macphail, 50 at **Aros**, in service with the Campbell tacksman there. Colin was almost certainly the husband of Christian Macphail, and in 1786 they were to have "twains" Duncan and Colin to add to Hugh and Donald, seven and five in the census. At **Arle**, up the coast, in the 1779 census, Archibald aged 57 has two sons and a daughter, and John 40 has three sons. At Tobermory, John Macphail is an officer in **Baliscate** aged 55, with a son, Alexander, 15. Over at **Tenga**, there is a good number of Macphails, and the same at **Killimore** and **Achronich.** The Ross of Mull seems to be devoid of Macphails, while Torosay Parish has a few at **Kilpatrick**. When we cross the divide to Lochbuie rentals and papers of 1781, we find the Macphails who were the progenitors of the mid-19th century entrepreneurs. In **Rhoail, Bradil** and **Coiregairn**, Duncan, John, Angus, Donald and another John represent the family. Two or three are probably brothers, but as the Torosay baptism records do not begin until the 1790s, we are unable to tell. All we know is that Macphails born in Rhoall and Bradil were later to offer the highest rents for the best farms in Mull, and that they were either farmers of the highest acreages, or cattle dealers. Duncan Macphail and his son Angus (1816-1862), formerly in **Corrynachenchy**, moved about 1849 to **Cuilbhuirg** in Iona with their wives. Donald Macphail's(1746-1836) son, John, (1795-

1872) married Catherine Carmichael at **Grass Point** in 1831, farmed at Scallastle, then at **Tiroran**. Most of his children went to New Zealand. Another son, Duncan (1795-1876) was unmarried, and farmed 2,500 acres at **Garmony,** a nine-roomed house. A swift survey of the 1861 census shows Macphails in seven of the best farms in Mull and Iona. The best-known Macphail of all, the poet and author of *An t-Eilean Muileach,* Dugald Macphail (1818-1887) was the son of a different Donald Macphail and his wife Catherine Campbell. Dugald married Janet Merry in 1853, a girl whose father was one of the first incomer lowland farmers in Mull. Dugald became an architect to the duke of Westminster, although what this meant is hard to determine. He returned to Scotland for the sake of his children's education, and his children justified the move by being brilliant scholars. He gave talks on literature and history in Greenock and Glasgow, which were reported in the diasporic Highland press. His monument is at Lussafoot, said to have been built from the very stones of the house he was born in, a boast which seems to us today rather barbaric, since it would have been much more interesting to see his house!

I am being rather partial in allowing MacPhersons into this book, which is limited to the most current names in the early 19th century. MacPhersons had a very low profile in the last quarter of the 18th century, and I can find only one among the 1675 names. In 1779 the ducal census of Argyll lands has Lachlan MacPherson, 12, and his brother Alexander, 10 as sons of the deceased Donald MacPherson in **Tenga**. Their mother, Catherine Campbell is named, but their sister is not. Other MacPhersons in 1779 were John aged 30 at **Baliscate**, near Tobermory, and John MacPherson, 54, tenant in Corkamull with Neil, 16 and Donald, 3. Already one can see that MacPherson Christian names are not going to be illuminating. Another Donald MacPherson, born about 1778 is the only cooper who has appeared in Mull in the first half of the 19th century. He probably married Catherine MacPhail in about 1810. They had a Donald, a Catherine, a Robert, a Hugh and an Angus, and seem to have changed their abode several times between Glenaros and Kentallen. But the parents, Donald and Catherine, were still in the **Aros** area in 1851. A Hugh, born in Aros around 1810, and possibly the son of Donald the cooper, married an Ardnamurchan girl called Catherine MacKenzie and then moved to **Kinloch** at the head of Loch Scridain. Their first son Donald was baptised in 1841, but subsequent children who appear in the censuses, do not have baptisms, and it is very likely that Flora, Alexander, Margaret, Mary and the marvellously illuminating Louisa, all born between 1842 and 1859 came into a family that had either embraced the Baptist faith, or were early adherents of the Free Church. In 1883, when the commissioners of inquiry into the condition of the crofters and cottars in the highlands and islands visited Bunessan, Alexander, 40, was still a crofter in Kinloch. His testimony was an excellent piece of writing. He described Kinloch crofters as "half water half land plants, studded over the poorest part of the slopeland, often flooded by the tide". It was Alexander who gave the grisly evidence which hit the newspaper headlines about Neil Black (see under Black), and about Widow MacDonald who had maggots in her before she died. His manner of delivery was factual and courteous. If he was not carried shoulder-high by his fellow crofters, he ought to have been, but it was too late, and too many miserable Kinloch paupers had already died. Like John Campbell of Dervaig, Alexander MacPherson had talent which had very little outlet in his day, and he deserves to be made known to his clan.

MACQUARRIE

Australians will recoil to see this most revered name with a double r, but this spelling is the one which survived on the island of **Ulva**, and on Mull. Everyone knows that Macquarries came from Ulva particularly, and devotees of Samuel Johnson and James Boswell have a clear impression of one of the chiefs of the clan who greatly impressed them on the 16th of October 1773. But Governor Lachlan Macquarie had a more informed comment. Writing to Murdoch Maclaine of Lochbuie in 1801 about one of the old chief's sons, he said, "He is vain, ostentatious and extravagant to a ridiculous degree, and added about the father, poor unfortunate man, he is himself the primary cause of his family taking a wrong turn to all kinds of folly". No one quite understands the degree of kinship between the Governor-General of New South Wales and the foolish old chief of the clan, for Lachlan never spelt it out, although he was keen to use the family crest. The old man died landless in 1818 at the age of 103, and after his death, the Governor-General's brother Charles became the laird of Ulva's isle by purchase. He was a soft-hearted laird at a time when the island was staggering from the economic reverses which followed the collapse of the kelp industry, but his stewardship of Ulva was contemporaneous with his nephew Lachlan's ownership of the estate of Jarvisfield, and legend has often confused their roles. When Charles was laird of Ulva, 150 MacQuarries still lived on the island, being fruitful and multiplying as if there was no tomorrow. The one I am tempted to cite, because he must have a thousand descendants, is John MacQuarrie the schoolmaster who first married Margaret Campbell in 1801 and had seven children, then in 1825 married Anne MacKinnon and begat another seven. John died in 1855. But care must be exercised here, for there were three school-masters in Mull with the same name at the same time. What is extraordinary about the island of Ulva, about 5000 acres in area, is that the small townships of **Ormaig** and **Kilvickewen** held scores of MacQuarries, and even if you have no forebears of the name, you can visit the little hamlets in an afternoon walk on Ulva and still catch the last ferry. Look at every ruin and think of the family. In 1774 a Lachlan married Mary McIlreoch from Gometra. They lived at Kilvickewen with John, Hector, Catherine, Malcolm and Neil. In Ormaig a John and his wife Florence McArthur lived with Susan, Donald, Florence, John, Hector, Ann and Marion. These cottages are easy to imagine inhabited, but Ulva is full of spots where scores of people lived, places that had a name then, but not now. For the saddest thing is that the placenames have been removed from the maps, as if by order of Mr Clark, who evicted most of the people in the 1840s. However, all MacQuarries did not come directly from Ulva. Another Lachlan MacQuarrie (1818-1893), son of Captain Lachlan MacQuarrie and Mary Shaw, married, while he was the Chamberlain's clerk at **Ardfenaig**, Marion, one of the Ardalanish McIntyres. He moved to Tiree to be Ground Officer there in about 1852, and the children bear a wonderful array of combined MacQuarrie and MacIntyre Christian names - Murdoch, Duncan, Lachlan, Mary, Marion, John and Charles Nicol. A boat carpenter from Kilfinichen, Hector

MacQuarrie, moved to **Tobermory**, "a very poor family" according to the Highland and Island Emigration Society, who helped them to Australia on the ship *Panama* in 1853. Hector took seventeen years off his age in his application. The best account of the MacQuarries is *Clan MacQuarrie: a History*, by R.W. Munro and Alan MacQuarrie.

A Mull branch of the Morisons seems to have been in **Penmore** from the sixteenth century. Whether or not they were connected to the bardic family of O'Muirgheasain is a question outside the scope of this work, but there are certain Christian names used by Morisons which suggest a connection, such as Muldony and Magnus. Penmore appears to have been the home of Morisons who bore those names, and Bellachroy, the name of the inn which served the Dervaig area before that village was built, contained a most interesting family in the 1790s and 1800s who probably were descended from the O'Muirgheasains. This was Charles Morison, who suddenly appeared in the Kilninian and Kilmore parish register about 1795 with his wife Margaret Maclean. Between 1795 and 1812, eleven children were baptised to them, Anna, Isabel, Lauchlan, Mary, twins Hector and Hugh, Neil, John, twins Allan and Roderick, and Magnus! Charles was in the 1841 census aged 70, with his son Roderick, now the publican of the Bellachroy inn. Further north on the Quinish headland, in Penmollach dwelt, in 1841, Donald Morison, 60, with his wife Janet Rankin and only two of their children, Lachlan, 20 and Catherine, 14. We know from the parish registers that they had at least seven children, and that one of them, Neil, born in 1811, later became known as Neil Rankin Morison. Neil's son was the antiquarian, Counnduillie Rankin Morison (1856-1943). I am fairly sure that all these north west Mull Morisons had links with the bardic family, but of course they are impossible to prove. The name was also represented in the Ross of Mull, Ardmeanach and Iona in the 18th century. A Farquhar Morrison in **Burg** was 88 in 1779, and therefore born in the 17th century. Duncan Morrison, tenant in **Iona** was born about 1730. His three sons, Neil, born about 1763, Hector 1767 and James 1772 may have carried on the line in Iona and the tip of the Ross of Mull. But a John Morrison in **Kilvickeoun**, south of Bunessan, who was 64 in 1779, also had a son James, born about 1764. Another John Morrison in **Ardtun** in the 1851 census, born about 1800, married Catherine Lamont in 1829 and had nine or ten children, including a James, who was four days old when the census man came round in 1851. In the two-roomed house, the 44-year-old mother was attended, during her confinement by her sister Mary Lamont, while John, a farmer with eight acres, and eight children, John, Hector, Archibald, Malcolm, Mary, Marion, Duncan and Robert, had to answer the enumerator's questions. The fertile Catherine died at the age of 83, in Ardtun. Perhaps all these Jameses were named after the same forebear as James Morrison (c.1766-1828), who married Janet Maclaine in Uisken in 1814. James was a merchant in **Bunessan**, and Janet probably belonged to the prestigious Maclaines or Macleans of Uisken. She was certainly well educated, was called upon to read and write letters, and was referred to as "Mrs Morrison" - a mark of respect in a world where she would normally have been called Janet Maclean to her dying day. James's tombstone at Kilvickeoun tells us that he was drowned in the Sound of Iona on 2 May 1828, and therefore he left perhaps seven children and the posthumous Jemima. Posthumous children were always given the father's name if a boy, and a feminine version of it if a girl. After the sudden death of her husband, Janet sought asylum with her sister Catherine Fletcher at Tiraghaoil, but later returned to Bunessan, where her descendants lived at Rhumore (where you can now have bed and breakfast) until the turn of the 20th century.

The first thing that must be said about the name of Rankin is that it is **not** one of the most frequent names in Mull at all, although, rather like Beaton, it is a name that is associated with the island because of some famous ones - in this case, the hereditary pipers to the clan Maclean. My second *volte face* is that this time people who have Rankins in their tree might be allowed to venture, most tentatively, to think that they **are** related to the family of pipers. It is certainly not a general name in Mull. There were no Rankins whatsoever in the Argyll estate lists (and remember those were successors to the Duart lists), and none in the Lochbuie lists in the 18th century. Instead, it will give you a little frisson to realise that they are only in the **Kilbrennan/Tostary/Kilninian** corner, and that this is because, with their masters, the Macleans of Duart gone into a lengthy exile, they left the forsaken Duart Castle for Torloisk, in other words for the Macleans of Torloisk who had put on the mantle, and looked after the legal affairs of the exiled chiefs. The Torloisk Macleans were not, of course, as grand as the Duart Macleans had been, even when the Duart chiefs were immersed in debts, and it is not clear that any ceremony at Torloisk (then a humble thatched house) would have been an appropriate theatre for the talents of the Rankins. They were probably simply given asylum on Torloisk lands. Rankins did not have only one piper, but so infectious was their love of music that many sons, and even their wives, could tease the pipes into producing beautiful sounds. Some Rankins went to the Torloisk Macleans, some to the Coll Macleans and some to the Muck Macleans. Dr Johnson admired the piper, John Rankin in Coll in 1773, and the same man was mentioned as being on the Quinish estate in north-west Mull in 1752, which also belonged to the Macleans of Coll. In **Kilbrennan,** a 'college' of piping flourished under Counduillie Rankin in the 17th century, followed by Hector, his son, and Hugh **his** son, with the teaching coming to an end around 1760. But Hugh or Neil Rankin probably taught Archibald Macarthur, piper to Ranald Macdonald ("Staffa"), in Ulva, "Duncan Piper" who played for the Lochbuies, and Neil Maclean, who stirred the 84th regiment at Halifax, Nova Scotia in 1782. Neil Rankin (c.1750-1819) removed himself and his family to Coll, and his sons Hector and Counduillie emigrated to Prince Edward Island in 1820. Working on the hunch that any Rankins in Mull after

1820 were connected with the pipers, we may assume that a remnant was assimilated into Mull families. Janet Rankin, daughter of Neil Rankin, married in 1809 Donald Morison, and lived in **Penmollach**, and their son Neil, born in 1809, was the father of the Mull antiquarian Counnduillie Rankin Morison, who died at Strongarbh House, Tobermory in 1943, aged 87. Catherine Rankin, the redoubtable midwife of the small islands of **Gometra** and **Little Colonsay**, may have passed on hints from the breathing techniques of pipers to her women in childbirth. She had herself a son named Finlay, a recurring Rankin Christian name. Several Hector Rankins suggest direct descent from the main line, one of them marrying in 1794, Mary Campbell, and living in the Kilbrennan "Rankin country". Another Hector Rankin, born about 1810, lived on the island of Little Colonsay in 1851, farming eighty acres of land. The 1871 census of Mull yields only three incomer Rankins and a sixteen-year-old herd from Kilninian in Glenforsa with the great old name of Hector Rankin. Whether this boy was the sole blood representative of those who once piped in the halls of the chiefs is yet to be discovered.

A curious name which is strictly speaking not one of the commonest names in Mull, but so much is it tied to a particular area in the Ross of Mull that if this little book travels anywhere, and finds a Rose, it should cause much happiness. Of course there are real Roses, from Kilravock, in the north east of Scotland who may have been the ancestors of our Mull Roses, but it is rather nice to think of a Ross branch of Roses! The patriarchal figure seems to have been Alexander Ross, tenant in **Saorphin** in the duke of Argyll's census of 1779. Alexander was 70, and his only son David only 16. Alexander's wife is not named, but she had four maids, which is quite a lot for a family of three. You might think that **Ardchiavaig** is quite far from Saorphin, but in those days a track linked Shiaba and Scoor and Saorphin to Ardchiavaig. In Ardchiavaig, in the same census, dwelt Donald Ross, tenant, 53, with sons William, 13, Archibald, 11, and Donald, 8. There was a wife, and two daughters, and a servant man, John McLucass. This too seems a prosperous family. These were all the Roses in Mull. How they came there I do not know. But in 1785, another Rose, Eugene, was born at Killiechronan, or perhaps it was 1780 (the date is derived from Eugene's death in 1855). Eugene seems a delightfully decadent and stylish name for Mull. In Gaelic it was Uisdean. In 1817 we find him in **Suidhe**, near Bunessan, marrying a girl from Tiree called Flora Sinclair, who of

course, on her marriage, would be Flora Rose. By 1831 Eugene and Flora had Catherine, Donald, Mary, Ann, Alexander, and twins Neil and Annabella. William Rose who was 13 in 1779, later had a natural son Alexander Rose, who married Marion Black, and had children in **Iona**. Eugene's father, David Rose and his wife Catherine Macdonald lived in Suidhe having at least four other children, John, James, Annabella and Mary. James Rose, (1797-1874) married Marion Maclean in Ardfenaig in 1836, when he was an agricultural labourer and she took in washing, but somewhere about 1845 he became the beadle, and from then on was called by this name alone - Seumas Am Maor. It is difficult to establish the cousinly relationships of the Roses, but they all used the same Christian names. A second Eugene, born in 1804, lived in **Ardtun**, and was a boat carpenter. He was a Gaelic poet, and wrote a *Lament for the Factor Mor* (the duke of Argylls hated agent at Ardfenaig) which was in fact deadly satire. He remained unmarried, living in Bunessan with his mother, Mary Rose. Hugh Rose, a shoemaker in Tiree in 1851 was a Mull man. Isabella Rose (c.1787-1831) married Donald Macphail, a miller in Bunessan. She was the mother of Lachlan Macphail, (1827-1882) a merchant in Bunessan who married Mary Macphail in Glenbyre in 1867, daughter of John Macphail and Isabella Stewart. Ann Rose (1833-1921) was born in Iona, daughter of Alexander Rose, tailor there, and married Dugald Stewart. They are both buried at Lovat, Bruce County, Ontario.

Almost the only Stewarts in Mull at one time, but a family who were of great importance to the economy of the island, were the Stewarts of Achadashenaig, a farm which, in the mid-19th century, had its name changed to **Glenaros**. The house can be seen from the road near Aros Bridge, and was, in the 18th century, part of the Argyll estate. The Stewarts began by being Mull cattle drovers, and by good management, had turned themselves into respected tacksmen by 1763. The French writer and traveller, Faujas de St Fond describes having breakfast in 1784 with the Stewart brothers and their two intelligent and industrious sisters at their "commodious habitation on a small hill". As tacksmen to the fifth duke of Argyll, the brothers Robert and Duncan Stewart ran a large farm which extended as far as Oskamull, and before the days of roads, a track, which can still be followed most of the way to Killiechronan, connected the Sound of Mull with Loch na Keal. With such communications, Stewarts married into families in Oskamull, Corkamull and Killiemor. Allan Stewart of Achadashenaig married Mary Fletcher of Glencannel in 1794. Miss Catherine Stewart married Mr Robert Maxwell, Chamberlain of Tiree in 1818, creating a new layer of middle class society in Mull, which had tended to be polarised between gentry and commoners until then. In 1826 a Mr Charles Stewart married a Miss Margaret Carmichael in Torosay. Whether the schoolmaster, Dugald Stewart, born about 1780, was one of the drover family is hard to determine, but his daughters passed on the name of Stewart to their children as a matter of pride. Isabella Stewart of the Achadashenaig family, born about 1800, married the Morvern landowner Dugald McLachlan, in 1823 and lived in Killiemore House at Kilfinichen. Her daughter Catherine was later to marry the heir of Francis William Clark, the laird of Ulva, who became notorious for evicting about six hundred Ulvaichs. Catherine's husband predeceased his father, and so never inherited the island. Isabella Stewart, daughter of the schoolmaster, married John McPhail in 1835. The Stewarts, in the person of John Stewart, son of Robert, succeeded James Maxwell as Chamberlain of Mull about 1830. Another John Stewart was briefly tenant of Inchkenneth in the 1860s. Lachlan Stewart was a troublesome tenant in Glenbyre in 1818, who caused some anxiety among the heritors, or landowners, as he had the unpleasant habit of destroying his house when his lease expired. Some tinsmiths, or tinkers, named Stewart peddled their wares in the 1840s, and stayed on in Mull. But the main line of Stewarts, probably all connected with the upwardly mobile drovers, were in farms under the original jurisdiction of Achadashenaig or **Glenaros**, such as **Corkamull, Oskamull, Acharonich** and **Killiechronan**, with a ship carpenter, Alexander Stewart at **Ardchoirk** near Loch Don, and Anne Stewart, wife to Duncan Carmichael making up the Torosay branch. The Hugh Stewart who married an Iona girl, Grace McFarlane, in 1838, appears to have come from Tiree.